PEOPLE

People

ESSAYS & POEMS

EDITED BY

SUSAN HILL

CHATTO & WINDUS

THE HOGARTH PRESS

LONDON

Published in 1983 by
Chatto & Windus · The Hogarth Press
40 William IV Street
London WC2N 4DF

British Library Cataloguing in Publication Data
People.
1. Biography
I. Hill, Susan
920'.02 CT101

ISBN 0 7011 2637 X

Printed in Great Britain at
The Camelot Press Ltd, Southampton

Contents

5

Contents

Illustrations

All these works are in the Ashmolean Museum, Oxford.

Acknowledgements

The editor and publishers gratefully acknowledge permission to reproduce drawings from the Ashmolean Museum, Oxford, and to reprint copyright material as follows:

Bernard Shaw: from *Heartbreak House*. Reprinted by kind permission of the Society of Authors on behalf of the estate of Bernard Shaw. John Stewart Collis: from *The Worm Forgives the Plough*. Reprinted by permission of the author and Penguin Books Ltd. John Betjeman: 'Colonel Kolkhorst.' Reprinted by permission of Sir John Betjeman; from 'A Hike on the Downs' from *Collected Poems*. Reprinted by permission of John Murray (Publishers) Ltd. Frederick Treves: 'The Case of Sir Henry Irving.' Published by kind permission of the President and Council of the Royal College of Surgeons of England.

Introduction

In 1981, a splendid anthology of topographical essays, poems, photographs and pictures was published, under the title of *Places*, by Oxford University Press. The editor was Ronald Blythe, and all profits were donated, by contributors and publisher, to Oxfam.

So successful and highly praised was *Places* that a second book was immediately mooted. Various topics were proposed, and I was invited to be the editor, a task I was more than happy to undertake, though I was very conscious indeed of the difficulty of following in Ronald Blythe's expert footsteps.

But I was not entirely sure that the suggested subjects for the collection could be made to work as a whole. What I was casting about for was one single, simple idea on which to focus the anthology, something with a clear and obvious point, yet which was capable of containing a wide variety of contributors' points of view. I am indebted to my husband, Stanley Wells, who then said, 'Well – after *Places*, why not *People*?' Of course! The idea was exactly right, I recognized it at once, and so, I'm glad to say, did Hugo Brunner of Chatto & Windus, the book's publisher, and Guy Stringer and Stephanie Ross at Oxfam. It is the right idea for many reasons, and not the least of these is the fact that the chief concern, indeed, the whole *raison d'être*, of Oxfam is 'People'.

I wrote to a great many, very different kinds of men and women, asking if they would consider writing something for the book, and I suggested that they might choose as their subject someone, anyone at all – dead or alive, famous or unknown – who had been in some way influential in their lives, made a great impact upon them, helped to mould some aspects of their lives, careers, personalities, beliefs. But I also decided to welcome any more general description of 'a person'.

No one, among those who so generously agreed to contribute, seemed to have much difficulty in deciding upon their subject. Many said that the person 'chose themselves'. They are all, like the writers, very different people, though certain types recur: schoolteachers are an obvious, important influence and great newspaper characters have made a decisive impact upon aspiring young journalists. But each piece seems to me to be utterly itself, a vivid pen portrait of a unique individual, and an explanation of his or her memorability. The portrait drawings used to illustrate the book were selected after considerable help and guidance was generously given by David Blayney Brown and Noelle Brown, both members of the staff of the Ashmolean Museum, Oxford. My thanks are due to them for their help and advice.

The essay by Sir Frederick Treves is, like all other contributions, published for the first time in this book, but its author, known to many people for befriending 'The Elephant Man', died exactly fifty years ago.

I am more grateful than I can express to all those whose warm response made my work ultimately so rewarding. *Their* reward, I hope, will be the knowledge that they have performed a valuable act of generosity towards a charity which provides the very essentials of life, and therefore, and above all, hope for a future, to the hungry, the oppressed, the persecuted, the maimed and the destitute of this benighted world.

It has been a great privilege to be associated with such a fine collection of People.

SUSAN HILL, Oxford, 1982

People

The Ninetieth Birthday

SVETLANA ALLILUEVA

She was sitting in her favourite chair near the large window, overlooking the lake and the wide, pale open winter sky. Blinding white snow lay everywhere: it had made her put on dark glasses. Birds were fussing over their food on the open porch next to the window, including a red cardinal, regal and proud among them all. A grey squirrel darted about boldly and grabbed sunflower seeds from in front of the nose of the cardinal.

The lady was sitting very straight, keeping her neck up, her shoulders broad, her arms round like a ballerina, with her hands together on her lap. Her feet in dressy low-heel shoes were crossed comfortably. She was looking at the birds outside, recognizing each one of them. She had enjoyed that silent winter contemplation at this window for twenty-five years.

That day she was dressed in a long beige velvet skirt, soft and informal, and a chiffon blouse with long sleeves, beige too, with big red flowers and green leaves on it. She enjoyed the costly simplicity of this festive outfit – there was a good reason for wearing it. Her hands with thick veins were composed on the soft velvet of the skirt; her large grey eyes were watching birds. A half-smile of inner peace was touching her lips, her cheeks cut with deep long lines, her face all wrinkled, but her eyes bright and quick.

She had been quietly enjoying the afternoon after a big noisy dinner the previous night, when her sons, grandsons, great-grandsons and their wives, about thirty-five people altogether, had taken her out for a big family celebration of her ninetieth birthday. They had all appeared suddenly in this small town with flowers – her son from Massachusetts, her daughter from Connecticut, another son from New Jersey, a daughter-in-law from Colorado, and their families – it had been planned so long ago, secretly – and in the evening they had come to pick her up from her small house on the lake, where she lived alone. She had been driven to the local Club, taken over for the occasion by this crowd of well-dressed, well-to-do men and women, whom she loved, had brought up, educated and patiently followed from a distance for years, never imposing on them any parental rigidity. She had given her children what she cherished so much, but did not have much of in her own youth – total independence and the freedom to think and make choices and decisions. 'I never wanted to mould them into something the way I have been moulded,' she would often say. She gave them all so much of herself that by now warm waves of love were returning to their native shores – to her. She knew the process, enjoyed it immensely, and her old days were, therefore, days of fulfilment. Even so, she loved to live alone, with the occasional company of a visitor, a house-guest or of a grandchild, but most of the time alone and independent. 'I cannot let them run my life,' was her motto. And the philosophy of a lifetime.

Now she could relax, put her hands quietly on her lap and silently listen to the soft pulsating of warmth around her. She was a happy person, and she knew that.

Several neighbours and friends walked in, brought more flowers and sat down with her near the big window. They all smiled, admiring her good looks, her posture, her dress. 'But I do not feel old!' she said, as if apologizing for her age. 'I do not know why, but I do not feel that I am ninety years old!' she laughed. A young woman in blue jeans answered: 'That is probably because you were never afraid of getting old. Nowadays everyone is horrified of ageing when they are only thirty, no! when they are twenty!'

'Yes, maybe you are right,' she answered. 'I was never afraid of becoming older, because, I think, I was aware of the advantages of old age. I have always loved to look back on the past and to enjoy what has been done, what has been lived through. What is there to be frightened of?'

The young woman laughed, trying to visualize herself in her own eighties. She found that funny and incredible, and kept laughing somewhat nervously, as if she was looking deep down into a dark abyss. The hostess alone looked feminine among the others in the room. She touched her white hair, fingered her chignon with her hand to be sure that everything was all right. She disliked untidy hair-styles, but would never say so to those whose preference was different. Then her arms went back into her usual posture with a slow round movement, and the circle was completed once more on her lap.

She reached out with her finger to touch the earth in the flower pot with yellow chrysanthemums, then got up not without difficulty. Her arthritic knees bothered her. But she walked to the kitchen and brought a small watering can and poured some water on the flowers. 'Now,' she said, 'they will love it.' Since she was already on her feet she moved slowly around to give more water to a large pink poinsettia, to a spider-plant and to a camellia with several white flowers in bloom. They all stood around her armchair, and she loved their silent company.

Books and magazines were next to the flower pots, also close to her chair from which she observed the lake and entertained her guests. It had been like this for many, many years.

She had been born into a large family in the American Middle West, in a small town, where life was in those days, one might say, very provincial. Her hard-working family, where service to others had been cultivated by her strict and powerful mother, were an example to her. They did not know poverty, but they all had to work hard to avoid it. And helping the poor and the less fortunate had been a must. Her father had come from England. He had started a business in that town, which grew rapidly, as did his family. They used to hire young people from Europe to help in the household, and these young ones received good training together with the rest of the family. It was a simple, healthy life under the laws of the Presbyterian Church, to which she belonged all her life.

15

Through the Church she had learned early how to reach others with naturalness and to understand their needs without false effort and useless talk. She was a born humanitarian, and surely would have become a nationally known figure in that field if her own family and children had not become the centre of her life quite early on.

Her own young family did not escape pain and tragedy. One of her six children had died in an accident and she could never forget that little girl dying. Another daughter had to be placed in an institution for retarded children: this made her mother feel forever guilty. The most severe pain had been caused by the divorce, for which she had decided to file at a time when a divorce was still a very rare and extreme event. And she had truly loved the father of all her children.

A young Presbyterian minister at the time of their wedding, bright and openminded, he had gradually adopted views too liberal and extreme for her to agree with. He had become a patron and promoter of the early nudist movement in America. She had watched the development of this interest at first with patience, hoping that somehow he would soon abandon it. But he had grown more and more absorbed with 'naturalness' in every form, and eventually the nudist colonies had become the major cause of his life. It had not been easy at all for her to decide on divorce; but to accept the unacceptable had been truly impossible for her.

He had soon remarried, after that, and later she had remarried too, but had soon become a widow. After that she continued to live alone. Her former husband had not seen her for decades, neither had he wanted to.

They had met again after forty years. Accompanied by their children and grandchildren he had come to visit her at this little house on the lake.

'He was very nice. We were sitting on this terrace, the lake was so peaceful in the evening. It was lovely. What was it we could not agree about? – I thought. Then it grew dark, we went into the living room and the fire was started. He looked at the shelves loaded with books, then suddenly turned, began to talk, and became as difficult as he used to be long ago. He had not changed a bit. Neither had I, I guess.' She loved to tell this story.

She had been faithfully visiting him in the nursing home where he had been placed after a stroke. He had died there when he was almost one hundred years old.

The large family had gathered for a memorial service at home. It had been informal, because among their children there were Unitarians, Presbyterians, Quakers, Episcopalians and agnostics as well. Everyone had expected her to say something, and she had. She had spoken of him with warmth as if they had never been apart. She had spoken of his strength, dedication, his perseverence in serving others the way he saw fit. 'He opened wide my own horizons,' she had said. 'I have learned so much thanks to him.' She had made everyone feel as one family, stronger than ever, and they had all cried while she spoke.

Now she was even more alone than before, and she kept no ill feelings about the past. She felt good about her whole life, about her divorce, about her husband who died loved and remembered. She had a good feeling about herself and others, and it was good to be ninety. Her visitors in this room admired her and envied her, because they did not have that self-respect and self-assurance she possessed. It was the result of her deep faith in God and His goodness; but she never liked to assert that. She was a doer, not a preacher. Her visitors loved her, she was their adviser and their hero.

I first met her on some insignificant social occasion soon after I came to live in the USA and had settled in her town. She won my heart immediately and easily. Having lost my mother when I was six, I was forever looking for motherly warmth, and always loved old people. But she was more than that – she became my dearest friend. She was never too tired to listen, forever understanding, and never bossy. She used to listen like no one else, with her whole being; she would sit silently for a while, then her slow speech would start. I never heard her chatting or gossiping, or being mean about others; there was always dignity and authority in her carefully chosen words, and she possessed a good sense of humour, too.

I shared with her the joys and excitement of my first years in America, when my books were published and warmly received if not by all the critics, then certainly by the readers; my idealization of the free society, romanticism and enthusiasm with which I had stepped on these shores. I talked with her about the pain of separation from my adult son and daughter, and later from my newborn grandson; I did not have his picture because communications with me were forbidden by the Soviet government. Later, when I got married and lived on the West Coast, her Christmas letters and Easter cards would follow me everywhere.

Then came a tragic divorce from a man whom I loved deeply, but whose way of life in an artistic commune I was unable to accept. I returned to her small town with a year-old daughter, and sad years of secluded life followed. Tied at home with a baby, lonely and depressed with my failure, I did not hesitate to bring to her my disillusionments. She saw me turning from a cheerful idealist into an unhappy, bitter woman, and ageing too. I began to see clearly that the 'culture' of television, of clichés, of superficiality in knowledge and in relationships was as upsetting to her as it was to me. But, while I was constantly distressed and emotional, she had a seasoned vision of a patient, wise outlook. And she tried continuously to breathe into me her own realism, stability and good practicality.

She was a rock. Her health, stamina and profound faith in the justice of God were unshakeable. Her influence was that of healthy mentality, which is always infectious. She nurtured my point of view on age and ageing. Indeed, being with her even for short visits could not help but make me feel the harmony of mature and ripe years – not fear.

Neither was she afraid of death. 'I am ready to go, I am ready,' she would say. 'I do not know why God is not taking me, my work has all been done. I am thinking of death as a new experience, an important and interesting one; surely not as the end of the road. I am looking forward to it with curiosity.' She spoke as ever without sentimentality and affectation, and her words never sounded like a sermon. One could not help but trust her sincerity.

Emotional as always, I came to love her house, her rooms, the trees and shrubs of her garden, her lake, her kitchen – simply because they were hers. But at the same time I kept forever struggling to remain free and independent of other personalities: and she was the one to understand that better than anybody. She was not a possessive mother, nor a pushy friend, nor ever a vain woman. I think of her as of a born teacher, who leaves her pupils free to try their own wings.

Through those years of discovery of my new country, years of joys and pain, illusions and disappointments, losses and growth, through the rough times of finding my own new life in the stormy ocean of the free world she was my rock of stability. And when I think of her and of her life, I know how deeply, after all, I appreciate and love America.

J. R. L. Anderson

EDWARD BLISHEN

I was an amazed journalist aged eighteen when I first met J.R.L. – John – Anderson: who was then a journalist – as it seemed to me, of classic coolness – aged about twenty-six. I was on this really rather absurd weekly, the *Muswell Hill Record,* which among local newspapers was like some mobcapped woman leaning in the style of the cartoons of the day against a fence, gossiping to the mobcapped woman next door. The *Record* did not so much offer news as rattle and natter locally, in erratically printed columns ruled off from one another by very black lines. John Anderson was on our rival, the *Hornsey Journal,* a tabloid in format but not in substance: written, always with literacy, often with wit, by a team most of whom were in their twenties. Something of the feeling I then had for . . . W. H. Auden, D. H. Lawrence, John Donne – a whole cloud of great remote cronies, who included any contributor whatever to the *New Statesman* – I also had for the *Journal.* There was something incorrigibly daft about local journalism, but the *Journal* team were, as I saw it, being rather stylishly ridiculous now so that they could be gravely famous later. I thought they were all on their way to being renowned novelists, poets . . . contributors to the *New Statesman.*

A journalist was not at all what I'd hoped to be. By the grammar school I'd been headed, but awfully uncertainly, towards university . . . Oxford, it seemed: but the school's doubts, great though they were, were nothing to my own. Briefly, my father was against it, and I must have been against it myself, somehow, because I did nothing to make myself ready for it. Instead, I did much to ensure that I was perfectly unprepared: not reading set books, but reading novels – except where a set book *was* a novel, when I read some other set book that didn't happen to be in our syllabus. I think my particular experience as a first-generation grammar schoolboy, added to frailties of personality all my own, had made me at one and the same time dream most intensely of going to Oxford, and scheme most intensely to prevent it. A measure of the desirability of Oxford was that it was not for me. Something like that.

So, in Muswell Hill, I met John Anderson. He was very tall, and very thin, and dressed always in pale grey. *He'd* been to university all right – though it was London. For some reason I felt this represented a splendid puritanism in him. Oxford and Cambridge were beautiful and romantic beyond words: but, equally beyond words, London was earnest and austere. (It was because of London, I think I felt, that John Anderson dressed with such complete absence of colour.) His face was lean, keen, hungry, and he had a voice – thin, exact – that seemed to lay words down as by the action of some rather fine printing press. When we walked to Highgate Police Court together, he loped: I longed not to walk with my own boring briskness, but with his strange, soft-footed bouncing stride. I associated his power over words with his manner of walking: the rhythm of his speech was exactly that of his long elastic pace. Every now and then, in the middle of some statement about poetry or politics, he would vanish. I'd look round startled and see that he was going back along the way we'd come. He'd have spotted a caterpillar, a beetle, any tiny thing, that was ill-advisedly using the pavement: would have picked it up, opened the nearest garden gate and deposited it in some safe green spot. John Anderson was always – in a fashion, I sometimes thought, that might have been difficult to explain to any challenger – bent double in gardens belonging to total strangers. Never once did I hear him speak of this frequently repeated activity. In the end you became accustomed and even addicted to it: his flow of intelligent words punctuated by tiny acts of rescue.

As it happens, I can't easily remember John's opinions, either as to poetry or as to politics: except, of course, in terms of his broad sympathies. But when I use the word 'broad', I see that what I really admired in him was what I felt to be a noble narrowness. He knew how, in a generous context, to make fastidious and even squeamish choices. I remember this with special reference to royal persons. An extension of a local hospital was to be opened by the Duchess of Kent, who was then only a year or so away from having been the beautiful Princess Marina. Opposed though I was to the royal principle, I had a feeling about the lady's looks allied to a secret sense of pity for a princess dowsed into being a duchess. On my way to cover the event, I ran into John Anderson, on his way from finding himself unable to cover it. 'Such falsity!' he groaned. 'Go if you must, but you'll find the place full of sycophants!' He was right about that. I enjoyed the scene, while supposing that I didn't: and looking back now, I see that John Anderson's sharply expressed abhorrence of it was part of my enjoyment. He was the first person I'd ever met who genuinely and on the best grounds both of sensitivity and philosophy, winced away from much that went on. As someone not yet aware how deeply he was drawn to the deplorable, the human muddle, I treasured his often quite dramatically discriminate sensibility.

I felt about him, I suppose, being myself so desperately astray, as a sort of signpost. He pointed in the direction of . . . some intelligent way of life. Intense, enormously difficult to satisfy, he thrilled me when I came under the friendly glare of his interrogation. I was reading . . . William Saroyan? What did I think of him? As part of my miserable preparations for failing the Higher School Certificate, and evading any possibility of a State Scholarship, I'd dodged making literary judgements of the faintest precision. In John Anderson's company, I took a first step towards the cheerful discovery, and acceptance, of my own opinions. If you failed to satisfy him, he was likely to lope away, at some speed – actually to quit your company and vanish. I learned a thing or two by way of being, from time to time, quite sensationally jettisoned by John Anderson.

How odd that I must describe this hero largely in terms of his dissatisfactions, and of what might seem a not wholly pleasing finnickiness. But much of the effect he had on me, and that I was greatly in need of, resulted from his sternness and touchiness. I remember the occasion of the concert that celebrated the raising of the pitch of the Alexandra Palace organ to a new international standard: which it was to enjoy for a year or so until a German bomb fell on it. The Great Hall was packed, but seemed less so than what one might have called the Great Platform: on which there were, for instance, the members of a choir a thousand strong. When they came to that sudden stop in the Hallelujah Chorus, the effect on the audience, I'd be ready to believe, was actually physically dangerous: you were catapulted off a towering cliff of sound into neck-breaking silence. The audience was so closely crowded that I spent the evening with my knee jammed against the bottom of Margot Asquith. At the time I was in the middle of a foolish love affair: and the foolish lady, having agreed to come on my second ticket, did not appear. John Anderson was marvellously severe. 'Stupid creature!' He rang for his wife, who appeared almost at once. Afterwards we talked about Beethoven's Fifth, conducted by Sir Henry Wood as part of the concert. On such music, said John, embargoes should be placed. It should be allowed to be played once only in ten years. At all costs music of this order should be preserved against senseless repetitions. I, who was benefiting greatly from the senseless repetition of music on radio, was exhilarated by the thought that this might be the beginning of an actual campaign to bring about a moratorium on over-familiar great music. And I felt, again, wonderfully rebuked.

John Anderson was once pleased with me. I'd interviewed an old lady on her hundredth birthday, and wrote of her with loving astonishment. 'I wish I'd written that,' he said: and I've worn no laurel wreath like it. He became a *New Statesman* contributor himself: a piece, based on our experiences at Highgate Police Court, about the ease with which, forced to urinate in awkward circum-

23

stances, one might be charged with exposing one's person with intent to insult a female. I remember walking away with him from a local concert, some time in 1939: 'How marvellous it would be,' he said, as we made our way down a suburban road, 'if we could take off the front walls of these houses and see what's going on inside.' Later that year we chanced to be together when the newspaper placards read: NAZI-SOVIET PACT SIGNED. We could hardly speak: but John Anderson said at last: 'It's Heaven announcing union with Hell.' (Even he, I reflect, was innocent, in 1939.)

He became a distinguished industrial correspondent of the *Guardian*: and then an even more distinguished writer of thrillers. We met once at a *Guardian* literary lunch: large, swollen fellows, who eyed each other disbelievingly. I was more incredulous still when, recently, he died. My portrait of him here is not a portrait of John Anderson. It's a blurred view that a grateful boy had, long ago, of a remarkable man.

Sir Cedric Morris

RONALD BLYTHE

The notion that he changed somebody else's life would not have appealed to Cedric Morris, and he certainly cannot be said to have changed mine. Not in any full, re-directed sense, that is. Yet it would not be as it is now without him. Not quite. Our meeting not long after the war, myself very young and he entering upon the first of his various stages of a coherent, beautiful oldness, introduced a whole range of new attitudes and ideas to my existence which gave it just the right amount of carelessness it needed in order to survive. But no actual advice or preaching, needless to add. Just an unapologetic display of hedonism and regular work which said: go and do thou likewise. Why not? Quite a lot of artists and writers in the Suffolk villages all around were saying much the same thing, but Cedric Morris, with his own beginnings rooted in an especially attractive wilfulness, said it most eloquently. When he died in February 1982, after a curious sliding tumble through his overcoat to the brick floor on which we met thirty years ago, I thought, now there must be a gap, a great vacancy, the shattering of the first circle. But no, and for the simple reason that when people are in their nineties, as Cedric was, they stop taking up the full human space. 'He's not all there!' the village boys used to shout at some persecuted creature of their own age, and for some months past it was plain to me that, although he was in his chair at dinner, or trotting down the black staircases at Benton End, or cutting into the talk with all the old amusement and relevance, vital aspects of Cedric had already wandered off on their own devices, leaving us just enough of his personality to trick us into thinking that he was still all here and could be for ever.

He knew differently. Last Christmas, when the first deep snow had fallen, he said to me, 'Do they touch your sleeve like this?' giving a little attention-drawing pluck to his jacket. Well, they don't, to be honest. Not yet. But if I manage to live to be ninety I dare say they will. Except for being almost blind – we said our names as we kissed him – and except for having to let his beard grow in a blossom-white fringe, he had altered hardly at all. When we pieced together the ancient photograph albums he had torn up, the images of his early self grinned through the rents, proving that time had only done the expected surface damage, nothing more. The long-lastingness of the incorrigible element in him was particularly obvious.

I was taken to Benton End for the first time by James Turner, a poet who had come to live on the Suffolk borders in order to write and grow mushrooms. I remember the day vividly. It marked not only the meeting with Cedric but also my first understanding of the nature of the local artists and writers, viewed as a group. First that it was not a coterie in the St Ives sense, second that it was linked together with much historic subtlety, so that one was forever discovering past inter-connections. In any case, James Turner's friendship with Cedric, like that of John Nash and many more, was based more on horticulture than art and literature, and after a brief taking stock of me, Cedric led us out into the celebrated brilliance of his 'iris week', and I was initiated into a realm of flowers, botanical and art students, earthy-fingered grandees and a great many giggly asides which I didn't quite get. He had just inherited his father's baronetcy and this seemed to add to the comedy. The gardeners wove their way round easels propped up in the long grass and the artists, of all ages, painted peering visitors and dense foliage in the exuberant Morris manner. The doors and window-frames of the ancient house glared Newlyn blue and there was a whiff of garlic and wine in the air from distant kitchens. The atmosphere was well out of this world so far as I had previously witnessed and tasted it. It was robust and coarse, and exquisite and tentative all at once. Rough and ready and fine mannered. Also faintly dangerous.

'Well,' asked James Turner, as we drove home, 'what did you think?'

I thought I had never seen anything like it, the big scrubbed table and the wooden platters, the cool ochre room crammed with lustre and bold oils of seabirds, formidable women fatiguing the salad and discussing plants, knowing youths, candlelight and marmalade cats (one of the women was Kathleen Hale), wine, a single electric bar fire sputtering before an eighteenth-century bread oven and an overall feeling of spartan grandeur. This last impression owed much to Lett, who had lived with Cedric since 1919, and who was also an artist. It was Lett who actually ran the school of art, complaining mightily, though always producing from a chaotic kitchen the most delicious food and drink. Nor did his contribution end there, for having placed it before us – their meals in the gaunt Suffolk bakehouse were curiously stately – he immediately took up his next role, that of story-teller. The tales were either scandalously about himself or floridly about their travels and encounters, and were designed to shock and inform. If his facts were often inexact, his gist was transparent. Occasionally Cedric would step in and straighten out some curly bit of tale without condemnation or fuss, or with one of his bouts of glee. Lett talked through a big wicked smile like the wolf-grandmother in Little Red Riding Hood. With his large frame and rearing, scarred bald dome, a legacy from the Western Front, and his mocking courtesy, he made no bones about dominating the scene. Much, much later, sitting with him during his last illness, at ease and fond of him, I tasted little surges of regret about my early self which, contrary to what was generally believed, was neither prim nor charmingly shy, but steely in that non-giving sense in which the young frequently are steely. But even then, as the pair of old friends complained their way out of a world which they had taken every advantage of, and which they had greedily enjoyed, I still found difficulty in telling either one of them, and it should have been Cedric, how grateful I was that they had deflected me from too much safety.

It was inevitable that I should become the Benton End scribe, especially as Cedric's notion of written information was one wobbly line on a postcard, and Lett's was as following:

Cedric was born, of phenomenal vitality, on December 10th 1889. He was the eldest child of George Lockwood Morris of Sketty, Glamorgan (who, according to Burke, was descended from Owen Gwynedd, the last Prince of North Wales) . . . Bored and nonconformist in his father's household he made off to Canada. There he worked as a hired man on ranches in Ontario where the farmers seem rather to have taken advantage of his unusual energy and his naif ignorance of standard wages in the New World . . . Eighteen months later, he seems to have been studying singing at the Royal College of Music under Signor Vigetti, whose attempts at raising his light baritone to a tenor were unsuccessful. He determined to study painting in Paris.

. . . In Paris he industriously attended all the available *croquis libre* classes at the Académies la Grande Chaumière and Collarossi; Académie Moderne (under Othon Friesz, André Lhote and, later Fernand Léger); and was one of the first to enrol at the Académie Suédoise . . .

And so on, through gaudy Mediterranean travels, Cedric's membership of the London Group and of the Seven and Five (seven painters and five sculptors), his hand in founding the Welsh Contemporary Art Exhibitions between the wars, the settling down in Suffolk and the post-war plant-hunting, painting winter travels, which I also vividly remember, and finally Lett's attributing to his friend 'an unprecedented breadth of palette', whatever that might mean. But the herald-like proclamation with its emphatic Gallicisms is mentioned because it contrasted so completely with Cedric's own version of events, not in detail but in tone. The past was all a bit of a mumble to him. If you listened hard you might be lucky and catch a glimpse of it, but no sweep of scene and wilful goings-on, and heightened in French, as with Lett. The reason was simple. Cedric was a pagan who liked the sun on his back and the day's colours in his eyes, and the tastes and sights and sounds of Now. On a really beautiful afternoon at Benton End he could be seen lurking amidst the vast blooms he had brought to Suffolk from all over the world, virtually hugging the Now to him, his brown old face tilted a little skywards and his person defyingly, or helplessly elegant in the brown old clothes. A tour through the beds was learned and hilarious by turn, Cedric himself becoming quite convulsed by the habits of some plants and people. It was a curiously unoffending mix-up of sweetness and malice, a cocking a snook at conventions which had wilted long ago, due partly no doubt to earlier such naughty responses to them. Contrasting quite overwhelmingly with this merriment was a seriousness about art and humanity which had a way of pulling one up, of forcing one to be entirely truthful about what one said next. The passing in turn of brilliant specialist information (usually about botany), ideas on painting, escatology, wisdom, period camp and the most memorable individual-respecting tenderness created the kind of mercurial atmosphere which I — all of us — never quite got accustomed to. It was, of course, a perfectly unselfconscious bravura language belonging to the old bohemianism.

I was intrigued and entranced by Cedric's creature-like satisfaction with present time. It made his days so expansive that although he was visited to an alarming extent, an enormous amount of painting and gardening went on, apparently without interruption. When he was ninety he cursed God, whom he still took to be some ghastly Sunday misery from Glamorgan, for 'insulting' him with old age, but his sensuous basking in what pleasurable little treats each hour might provide continued to the last. Nobody has such a good time as a good-time puritan. Although so unlike him, I was drawn easily into his conspiracy of laughing judgements and solid work, although, alas, I was too much myself to achieve anything approaching his freedom.

He had exhibited regularly since the early twenties, with Lett and Gaudier-Brzeska in New York in 1926, with Ben and Winifred Nicholson, Christopher Wood (whom he taught), Ivon Hitchens, John Piper and the other members of the Seven and Five during the thirties, and both Wales and Suffolk had recently mounted retrospectives, but few artists could have done less to put their work on view. Seen standing amidst his landscapes, portraits ('not speaking but shrieking likenesses', as Raymond Mortimer called them), and flower pieces, the latter absolutely magnificent, a confrontation by vegetable hue and texture, shape and one almost adds scent which were nothing less than Cedric's notion of being alive in the world on a bright day, he acquired a quite awesome dimension which made even those of us who nursed white and ginger cats with him before the bar-fire hold back a bit. Standing beside him would be Millie Gomersall, his housekeeper for many years, ex-Fitzrovian and friend of the poet David Gascoyne during his pre-war Paris days, and herself restored to a kind of state by the unaccustomed finery which both she and Cedric had donned for the occasion. Although so countrified, Cedric retained much of the cosmopolitanism which Paris and Fitzrovia had given him. He perched in cities – 'When you took a room in Percy Street, you never asked for anything more than a table, a chair and a bed' – but luxuriated in an open landscape.

When the Tate Gallery celebrates him, it will be odd to stand amidst what will be the longest account of British post-Impressionism, as a single artist can give it, and not have it dominated by that rangy figure with its soft voice being so courteous and so improper by turn. Staring down at us will be, not only the company we shared at Benton End but the company before we existed, Anna Wickham, John Banting, Anthony Butts, Keidrich Rhys, Lucian Freud (his pupil), Rosamund Lehmann, Archie Gordon, Richard Chopping and Penelope Keith-faced women with names like Mrs Byng-Stamper. And the earthy Cedric geography of Umbria, Cornwall, Brittany, the Algarve, Mexico and Suffolk, none of it remote or exotic any longer, although in even the paintings of the sixties there is a quality which suggests that such areas of daily light and air and absorbing work take some getting to. Between the heads and the places will be the famous twenties birds, ravens, shags and herons,

30

and everywhere his flowers, opulent, glorious, yet even at their most blazingly coloured and translucent, rooted in the soil which he had pressed around them. 'Not a boring thing,' was his ultimate accolade – rarely bestowed – when he was shown a friend's garden, and it was what he managed never to have in his life if he could help it, a boring thing.

Mr Perry

JOHN CAREY

One of the things I have always disliked about William Morris is that he is rude (at the start of *News from Nowhere*) about Hammersmith Bridge. For those unlucky enough not to know it, Hammersmith Bridge is a dignified Victorian structure, crowned with small but ornate pinnacles, which joins Middlesex to Surrey. When I was a child it was a source of intense and unmitigated delight. For one thing, being a suspension bridge it wobbled when buses went across. There you would be, clutching a parental hand high over the Thames, when suddenly the pavement would shiver and dance beneath your feet as a double-decker rumbled by. My parents alleged this made the bridge safer, but that did not detract from the thrill – it only made it more scientific and intriguing. Then there were the gulls. At Hammersmith, of course, the river is still tidal. On a good day you can smell the sea. At the ebb, wide mud flats appear, and these would be covered, especially in stormy weather, with huge gulls. When you crossed the bridge, gulls would bank and glide above you, beneath you, and all around. If you held a piece of bread over the rail, they would swoop and snatch it from your fingers. This, though, required courage, and was, besides, regarded as a health hazard. You didn't know where gulls had been. So a safer idea was to take a bag of crusts and toss them in handfuls over the water. Instantly, you would be the centre of a screaming, fighting white tornado. If you didn't look out, they would come straight at you and tear the bag from your fist.

Crossing the bridge from Hammersmith to Barnes you could glimpse, beyond the riverbank trees and the towing path, the edge of a large reservoir. That was the start of Mr Perry's domain. There were eight reservoirs in all, tucked in under the south rim of the big bend in the river opposite Chiswick. If you turned right just over the bridge, at the Boileau Arms, and walked down Lonsdale Road, the reservoirs, with grassy banks between, would stretch away to your right, behind what must have been nearly a mile of green-painted railings. It was a scene I became used to, because I was born in a house halfway down Lonsdale Road, and my bedroom (it was really a small dressing room leading off my parents' bedroom) had French doors and a balcony looking straight out across the reservoirs. There were no buildings – just sheets of water, grass, gulls, and the distant trees marking the river. Beyond that you could pick out the tower of Chiswick church. Some of the reservoirs, so my parents said, were not strictly reservoirs but filter beds. These would be emptied periodically, leaving an expanse of fine sand at the bottom, a marine smell, and a good deal of green water weed, which men would rake into heaps and cart away.

Mr Perry was the Metropolitan Water Board engineer responsible for the site, and he had a cottage which stood, quite by itself, at the westernmost tip of the whole complex, opposite Harrods' playing fields. It had high gables, red bricks, green window frames (to match the railings), and a grass bank in front with concrete steps up it, a squeaky gate, and a neat flower garden. Behind, Mr Perry's vegetable garden extended – illimitably, so far as I could tell – in a series of square beds surrounded by grass paths. On Sunday mornings, after church, my father and I would visit Mr Perry. For me, the occasion always had a pleasantly ritualistic feel. Apart from anything else, there was the anticipation of Sunday dinner, with roast meat and potatoes, when we got home. Also, I was seldom alone with my father at any other time, but on this particular trip my brother and sisters never accompanied us – and my mother, naturally, was cooking the dinner. We were two men together – or three, if you counted Mr Perry. It was just after the war, and I must have been about twelve. The purpose of our visit was to admire Mr Perry's vegetables. Looking back I can see (though I never thought about it at the time) that the immaculate rows of peas and beans and cauliflowers must have had a melancholy appeal for my father. During the war we had lived in the country, where we had a big garden, and he grew all the vegetables the family needed. Now, back in the cramped suburbs, Mr Perry's patch was as near as he could get to his lost agricultural dream. That, I suppose, is why we went solemnly, week by week, in our Sunday suits, to watch the cabbages hearten up and muse upon the thickness of the leeks.

Mr Perry would always be digging when we arrived, in his tweed cap and blue Metropolitan Water Board overalls, with a pipe in his mouth. There would be hand-shakings, and a guided tour of the vegetables – no mere stroll, but a detailed scrutiny, with regular halts and warm debates. I, of course, said nothing. My father and Mr Perry spoke. Mr Perry had a Worcestershire accent – at least, that's what I was told it was – with hearty, long-drawn-out vowels that I found deeply fascinating. I cannot, as a matter of fact, remember a single thing that Mr Perry ever said. Just listening to the noise he made was enough for me – that, and the feeling that I was part of a select male band. Mr Perry's rolled-up shirtsleeves and weatherbeaten face helped to make the occasion manly and mettlesome. It occurs to me that I never saw him inside a building. We stood out there under the sky, surrounded by vegetables and reservoirs, and it felt like an adventure. Mr Perry was, I knew, different from the people I normally met with – though I could not have explained quite why. Even now I can't work out how it is that he has stayed so clearly just under the surface of my mind for all these years – a kind of reference point, or a personification of something which without him would disintegrate into sun and wind and shining water and tobacco smoke and Worcestershire vowels.

Was it that I had a romantic sense of his intimate contact with the life of plants? I honestly can't believe it. Like most children, I was bored stiff by nature. Appreciating Mr Perry's vegetables was strictly for the adults, so far as I was concerned. I was there to appreciate Mr Perry. I could scarcely, if put to it, have told a Brussels sprout from a French bean. When annoyed with my own children nowadays for their lack of interest in gardening, I find it salutary to switch back to Mr Perry's allotment and visualize again the undifferentiated green blur which vegetation then presented to me. So was it something in the social situation that made Mr Perry's company so gratifying? Did I feel it to be generously condescending in my father and myself to pose, Sunday-suited, beside Mr Perry and his spade? Maybe. But flattering though it is to one's adult cynicism, that explanation too lacks credibility. I know that some children are supposed to be wondrously sharp about class distinctions, but my recollections are quite otherwise. In that respect, as in others, I was an abnormally slow developer. As far as social awareness went I seem, on looking back, to have been permanently asleep – cut off from reality by a fog of self-absorption.

Perhaps, then, it was Mr Perry's gusto and joviality that made him so vivid: they aren't qualities you encounter much in a careful middle-class upbringing. Mr Perry stood out because he seemed blithely at one with his world. He was its centre, and its gulls and waterworks radiated round him. I remember how he would jerk back his head to laugh. Even the laugh had a Worcestershire accent. He was a happy man.

Or was he? I have often wondered since; particularly when I have thought of Mrs Perry, and how I must have seemed as a child to the two of them. For they had no children. Mrs Perry was pretty and elegant, in what I recollect as a vaguely Spanish way. She had black eyes and hair, and usually, I think, a black dress and white apron. She never came out into the garden when my father and I were there. So we would see her only when we stepped briefly into the kitchen to pay our respects. Between house and garden was a wood and glass lean-to porch, which rattled enviably with all its panes when you shut the door, and smelled of tarred twine. Was I, as a child, a reproach to their childlessness? Was that why I sensed a coolness in Mrs Perry? And was it – can it have been – why Mr Perry assumed such a jaunty manner when I was around, and threw himself so heartily into his gardening? Was it to show he didn't care?

I shall never know. But such doubts have helped to cloud my memory of him. So have the things which time has done. I grew up, and went away to do my National Service, then to university. One day on a visit to my parents I passed Mr Perry's cottage, and noticed that it was derelict, with corrugated iron sheets nailed across its windows. Mr Perry, I learned, had retired, and I think it was said to Worcestershire, but perhaps I have imagined that. The reservoirs, it turned out, were to be grassed over – no more gulls. St Paul's School had bought the site, and was going to cover the Hammersmith Bridge end of it with its new buildings. Time passed: my parents died. I no longer had cause to visit Lonsdale Road. But driving up it one day, past Harrods' playing fields, I glanced across to Mr Perry's cottage. It wasn't there: just grass, and a gap of sky. All that complicated life was now only a shadow in my mind. Even the place where it had happened had been laid bare. That, I know, is how life always vanishes. But in the case of Mr Perry and his reservoirs the universal process of transience had been, so it seemed to me, rather abrupt. At least it taught me to expect nothing else.

John Crow

DOUGLAS CLEVERDON

Crow (as he was always known among his friends) was a large, bulky man, with a bullet head that seemed disproportionately small for his body. He shared several characteristics with the barely-remembered E. H. W. Meyerstein – a Johnsonian presence, gluttony, a passionate absorption in scholarship, lodgings piled high with books in calf or sheepskin. Each had a physical handicap. One side of Meyerstein's face was paralysed. Crow had a spinal disability that obliged him to wear a kind of brace or corset. But while Meyerstein, ravaged by bullying and beating at Harrow, was obsessively interested in criminally-inclined adolescents, Crow had an enormous gusto and relish for the whole range of human eccentricity, whether manifested in Shakespeare's London or in Damon Runyon's New York.

I met both of them while I was a bookseller in Bristol in the thirties. Meyerstein was lodging near the church of St Mary Redcliffe while he worked on his biography of Chatterton. Crow (born in 1904) had gone from Charterhouse to study medicine at Guy's Hospital. Finding himself unable to face operating theatres, he went up to Worcester College, Oxford, with an exhibition in physiology. He and I were contemporaries at Oxford, and had one or two friends in common, but didn't meet until much later. Crow was the kind of larger-than-life character around whom myths accumulated. In later years it was believed that he had been a professional wrestler and a swimming champion. By his own account, after coming down from Oxford (having co-edited *Isis* with Peter Fleming), he became 'a chronicler of the Prize Ring': for some time the New York correspondent of *Boxing*, and later the London correspondent for several American boxing journals:

interspersing this with contributions to *Punch*. At one time he was editor of a Sunday newspaper.

When I met him in Bristol, he was a sporting journalist on the *Bristol Evening Post*. The *Post* had been lately established as a result of public outrage when a Press Lord took control of the two local evening papers and then suppressed one of them. Bristolians had a strong sense of civic pride and civic duty – as when, during a severe water shortage, a friend of mine visited the mansion of one of the Wills family, our local tobacco magnates. As she emerged from the lavatory, she encountered a flustered female Wills, who exclaimed, 'Oh, you haven't pulled the plug, have you? We only pull it once a day.' But that is a digression.

The crusade for the *Post* was led by a gentle, high-minded local journalist, Ronald Kidd, who was later involved in founding the Council for Civil Liberties. He might well have been pained by its present combativeness. The *Post*, I think, suited Crow, for it enabled him to stand around talking. On one occasion, as he stood benignly leaning on his large umbrella at a street corner, a motorist asked him the route to Gloucester. Crow immediately offered to conduct him, and inserting himself and his umbrella into the car conversed all the way to Gloucester.

Between the wars and before the blitzes, Bristol was a very agreeable city – homogeneous, the right size, architecturally pleasing, and with all the activities proper to it. For me, Crow provided an extra dimension. In his company everything seemed slightly more exhilarating. His conversation was trenchant, witty, and usually loud. He had a vivid imagination and a strong sense of humour; and his actions were often as unexpected as his observations – as when he and I were walking up Park Street, and the sound of traffic (not that it was much in those days) drowned something he was saying. He repeated the words, but I still could not catch them. He stopped before a haberdasher's window, breathed heavily over a large expanse of the glass, and wrote the words, as for a child before a blackboard.

For some years during and after the war I lost touch with Crow. Meanwhile I had moved to London, and married. Then I chanced to learn that he was now an eminent Elizabethan scholar and bibliographer, and was on the staff of King's College, London. I could hardly believe it. His normal conversation had shown that he was well-read, but there was never any hint that the boxing journalist might emerge as a specialist in Elizabethan bibliography. In due course we met again – it must have been some time before 1950, for clothes rationing was still in force (Crow had lately found in some village shop a stock of woollen shrouds for the Burial of the Dead, for which clothing coupons were not required. He had bought a couple to use as night-shirts, and persuaded his aunt to embroider a black skull and cross-bones on each). He told me that he had been declared unfit for war service, and had spent the war as an usher at Wellington College. He had not much enjoyed it, though several of the boys remained his friends. At the end of the war, then aged forty-one, he had got a job as a temporary assistant lecturer in English at King's College.

Crow remained at King's for seventeen years in a comparatively lowly post, which must have involved a fair amount of drudgery in the correcting of examination papers and so forth. It was not until 1962 that he was appointed Reader. During these years Crow amassed an encyclopaedic knowledge of Elizabethan and Jacobean literature – it was said that he knew by heart all the 26,143 entries in the *Short Title Catalogue of English Books, 1575–1640*. His erudition was of the wholly admirable old-fashioned sort, acquired for its own sake rather than to promote his own academic prestige or emoluments. So while the writings of his friends and colleagues frequently contained footnotes to the effect that 'I am indebted to Mr John Crow for this reference', he himself published very little, apart from occasional articles in learned journals or pungent anonymous reviews in the *T.L.S.* He was commissioned to edit *Romeo and Juliet* for the Arden Shakespeare, but never completed it – partly, I suspect, because of an innate tendency to perfectionism, and partly through his relish for good time-wasting convivial conversation.

He had a disdain for academics who rushed into print; A. L. Rowse was one of his *bêtes noires*. He was implacably opposed to intellectual arrogance, humbug, pedantry, over-simplification, and self-regarding subjectivism; these were his targets in a paper that he delivered in 1957 to the Modern Language Association of America, entitled 'Deadly Sins of Criticism: or, Seven Ways to get Shakespeare Wrong', from which may be quoted: 'The criticism of Shakespeare was formerly an attempt to give assistance to the young; now we are forced to use it to impress our elders. What started life as a crutch has come to maturity as a banner with a strange device. Editions of plays, allegedly for the young, are used as pass-keys for the doors of academic promotion.'

However incontrovertible this declaration may be, the words seem to reflect some degree of personal bitterness. Of course, Crow was a late-comer to the academic world; he never hesitated to say what he thought, and he may have trodden on influential toes. Nor did he bother to endear himself to his students, some of whom were probably, at that time, Leavisites. Some positively hated him; others were shrivelled by his sarcasm, and sensed that he considered they were not worth his time. It was odd, and sad, and by current theory unforgivable that it should have been so. But he was essentially a research scholar, pursuing knowledge for its own sake and not for ulterior educational motives. Even though lecturing was what he was paid for, I find his example refreshing at a time when museums and other repositories of learning are pressured to display their collections in a manner that eleven-year-olds can comprehend.

Apart from his erudition in bibliography and textual criticism, Crow was a learned lay theologian and patristic scholar. Staying in Sunderland, he was taken to Durham Cathedral, where the tomb of the Venerable Bede prompted a Crow Clerihew: 'The Venerable Bede / Left out the Creed / and two-thirds / of the Comfortable Words.' In London he was a (High) Churchwarden of St Mary le

40

Strand. When our second child was baptized at the still higher Church of the Annunciation, Bryanston Street, Crow was one of his godfathers. The godmother was a dear friend of ours, Phyllis Downie, an Edinburgh lady of impeccable propriety, a librarian and, like Crow, a member of the Bibliographical Society. Subsequently, during tea at the Society's meetings in Burlington House, Crow might be heard booming across the room at her, 'Have you seen our child recently?'

There was a certain mystery about Crow's habitations. For some time he had rooms in Sydenham. But he tended to 'perch' (his own word) on his friends for varying periods. In his last years he lived in one of the small Welsh hotels then surviving between King's Cross and the British Museum, much revered for his learning by a devoted Welsh landlady. He frequently went around with a large knapsack, giving the impression of a pilgrim of eternity with all his belongings on his back, ready to doss down wherever opportunity offered. Inside the duffle coat that he always wore were 'poacher's pockets', designed for books instead of rabbits, and convenient for teasing the armed guards who frisked him at the Folger Shakespeare Library in Washington. Food, I think, was a fairly constant preoccupation. He was known occasionally to take the precaution of stopping at a pub for a few sandwiches before going out to dinner: on one occasion being surprised by his young host who had come to the pub to get a bottle of wine for his entertainment. When he first came to dinner with us, my wife realized that his two or three helpings, prolonged by the conversation he generated, were enough to ruin the timing of the soufflé; so thereafter she settled for more solid puddings.

Presumably he had to be careful with his money. Occasionally a gift of books would arrive anonymously for his godson. On one occasion, when he was in the Westminster Hospital for several weeks, he commissioned a visiting friend to buy for him copies of Walter de la Mare's anthology, *Come Hither*, as Christmas presents for three or four godchildren. He had bought it on publication at seven shillings and sixpence. There was an explosion of rage when he learnt that he now had to pay thirty shillings per copy. His own collection of books was essentially a 'scholar's library', preponderantly scruffy and imperfect seventeenth-century editions of poets and dramatists. Fortunately it was kept together after his death, and is still available for scholars in the library of the University of Kent at Canterbury.

After three years as Reader in English Literature at King's, London, Crow was Professor of English in the University of Pittsburgh from 1967 to 1968. It would be interesting to know what kind of impact he made there. He was by now aware, of course, that he was regarded as an eccentric figure, and occasionally, I think, over-did it: on one evening peeing rather noisily and ostentatiously with the lav door open while the rest of us went in to dinner. But this seemed only a minor affectation in comparison with his conversational panache. Over the years, his countenance, earlier a round cherubic baby-face, had become rather owlish, as befitted his erudition. His various ailments failed to quash his characteristic gusto until his death in 1969, a day before his sixty-fifth birthday. There is an apocryphal story that he died roaring with laughter at a passage he found in a book in the Reading Room of the British Museum. I wish it were true.

J. G. Farrell

MARGARET DRABBLE

I first met Jim Farrell at a party at Olivia Manning's, shortly after I'd read his Booker-prize winning novel, *The Siege of Krishnapur*. At least, I think that's where and when I first met him, but as Jim and Olivia are, alas, both dead, there is no way of checking this memory. Nor would there have been any had they still been alive, as we talked about this once or twice and even then couldn't be sure. But it seems likely. Olivia gave excellent parties which were usually attended by an interesting mixture of old friends and new people who had caught her attention, some of whom rapidly moved into the old-friend category, for she had a great talent for intimacy. She was very sharp about people she didn't like and books she didn't admire, but she was equally quick to express her enthusiasms and admirations. She and Jim admired each other's work very much, and indeed their novels had qualities in common. They were both distinguished by an ability to describe major historical events – the Indian Mutiny, the Second World War, the Irish toubles – in a way that was tangential and personal, yet at the same time objective and detached. They were both serious workers, who, unlike some writers, spoke about the process of work as though it were one of the serious preoccupations of life, and through it they reached a kind of impersonality. The impersonality of art, I suppose. But as this piece is intended to be about personality, and as I have written about Jim's art elsewhere, I shall try to recall the personal things that his friends miss so much.

Jim, as others have remarked, was that not unusual paradox, an extremely sociable recluse. He lived alone, in the days when I knew him, in a small bachelor flat off Knightsbridge. It had a look of serious work about it, but could be (and frequently was) converted

43

into sociability by a select gathering of friends and a wonderfully cooked meal. The kitchen was tiny, and the wine was kept in the bathroom. From the kitchen would appear course after course of delicious food; into it would mysteriously disappear used plates and cutlery. When I got to know him better I used to disappear after them to see if I could help, but the sight of the precarious stacks alarmed me, and I didn't like to upset his system beyond the offer of washing up the soup spoons for pudding. How it all happened, and happened so smoothly, I cannot imagine. I always stayed far too late, as the talk was so good, and the room so intimate (i.e. small) that one could always hear what everybody was saying. There is a vivid description of these dinners in his friend Malcolm Dean's memoir, published with Jim's unfinished novel, *The Hill Station*; in this Malcolm (whom I certainly did meet at Jim's) pays tribute to Jim's culinary skills, and describes how Jim taught him to cook. I in turn can pay tribute to the excellence of Jim's teaching, as Malcolm is as good a cook as his tutor. Maybe some will find this emphasis on food frivolous, or possibly, in this context, tasteless, but obviously it wasn't only the food that we remember. It was the courtesy, the wit, the ability to make us all appear our better, not our worse selves. Those were truly civilized evenings; if civilization has a meaning, I would sometimes think to myself, then this is part of it. Indeed, on one occasion, as we drank the last bottle of a particular vintage, I recall that somebody commented on the death of civilization as we know it, and prophecies thereof, and we drank to the evenings we had had, in gratitude that we had known them. Wisely, as it turned out.

In other ways Jim was, I suspect, extremely frugal, and lived in austere simplicity. He bicycled around London, and indeed around the Continent on his holidays. One of the stories that I always enjoyed was his account of arriving at Cabourg in Normandy, in search of Proust's Baalbec; he wanted a meal, just one meal, in Proust's Grand Hotel, and had some difficulty in persuading the management that a man on a bicycle was a serious guest. It was in memory of this story that, in his footsteps and Proust's, I dragged my then small children off to Cabourg; I insisted that we took a taxi for the last hundred yards, although we had walked the rest of the way from the station, for it would not do, I said, to arrive at the Grand Hotel on foot, lugging suitcases. The hotel manager at that time was called Monsieur Parodi. Jim liked that.

One final point about food, before I move on to other matters. I myself am an extremely anxious and indifferent cook, surprised each day that potatoes do boil, that meat does roast, that salad dressing does mix (and frankly with reason, as sometimes these things don't happen, or not as I planned), yet I never felt any embarrassment about asking Jim to a meal. There was nothing competitive about his hospitality; one could offer him anything, and it would be received as though it were perfection. This in itself is a great art. I recall one night going back with him to our house after a publisher's gathering somewhere, and finding nothing presentable to eat at all; once more we resorted to a take-away from Curry Paradise. I asked Jim what he wanted to drink with it. He inspected the possibilities and chose Pernod, a drink which lingers dustily on the shelf for years. Pernod and chicken Korma. It seemed very much Jim, and he made it seem a treat. It was some quality of tact in him, some delicacy of friendship that one does not often encounter. He was the perfect guest, as well as the perfect host. My children, who think many of my friends are mad, loved him.

He was a very good raconteur; his stories, delivered with an air of slight surprise and disbelief, were airy constructs, whimsical fantasies, and most of them probably true, though one could never be sure. Once we were talking about the teaching of English literature, and I happened to remark that I'd once marked A-level papers, and that those of such a school had been uniformly bad. Oh, said Jim, smiling amiably, that was *my* old school. It took me years to discover that this was not in fact the case. In a sense, he reconstructed his past through art. In his version, he went up to Oxford as a rugger-playing Philistine, and would have remained

45

one had he not contracted polio, which confined him to a hospital bed for a lengthy period and turned him into a writer. One wonders what would have happened had it not been for the illness. He (like Olivia) was spared much formal acquaintance with Eng. Lit., as he read History, and his knowledge of literature was, by his own account, eccentric; he admired Richard Hughes and Malcolm Lowry, but claimed never to have read a word of Jane Austen. He told me that he'd once, long before we met, written me a fan letter about one of my novels, but again, he may have been joking.

His sudden and tragic death was a terrible shock to all who knew him, and a loss to literature. He had just moved to Ireland, and was by all accounts very happy there, in his new-style seclusion. He was drowned while fishing; his body wasn't recovered for some time, and for a while I nourished the hope that he had merely, fantastically, vanished, and would reappear one day, to tease us for our sorrow. But it was not so; he had truly gone. One does not make many such friends in a lifetime. His attitude towards women in his writing was odd, even hostile, but in life he was the easiest of friends, always ready to listen to tales of emotional disaster, with a kind of astringent sympathy that verged at times on outright criticism. I learned of his death in circumstances that I still recall with horror, and describe now in order to exorcise them. It was summer; I'd just got back from holiday abroad, and was looking over the newspaper at breakfast; I noted that the other J. Farrell, author of *Studs Lonigan*, had just died. Oh look, I said lightly, the other J. Farrell is dead. A silence fell, and then one of the children said that ours had just died too, and told me the story, in so far as it was then known. I didn't know what to do, think or say. It seemed impossible, and impossible that there was nothing to be done about it. The books are left, of course, but that's not enough, and he was in mid-novel when he died, which made things somehow worse.

For weeks I was so stunned I didn't shed a tear. Then, one night, I dreamed a dream. I dreamed that I was at a large party – probably one of George Weidenfeld's, for George published us both, and we often used to meet there. It was an oddly frightening party, full of people I didn't know, and many of them were sinister, changed half into animals, as in Circe's den; I was in a state of panic, looking around, as one does, even when guests aren't changed into animals, for someone I knew to speak to, when I saw Jim. He was wearing his white suit; he was always very elegant. I walked towards him, overcome with relief, reaching out my hand, and just as he was about to take it I remembered that he was dead, and he began to fade and recede from my sight. He was untouchable. But he was smiling, quizzically, and was so much himself, so vividly himself, unlike all the other people there: he shook his head slightly, and continued to smile, as I began to cry, and he said, very distinctly, 'It's all right, you know, it's quite all right.' And then I woke, weeping. But it was a good dream: I felt that I had truly seen him. I don't think I believe in a spirit world or an after life, but I do believe in the truth of some dreams, and that the past lives in the present. That morning I had a letter from Jim's mother; also, hoovering the carpet under the dressing table, which I rarely do, I found the lost last postcard he had sent to me, from Ireland. It all seemed to fit together; all these trivial things. There is no reason to it, but then such things are not reasonable. His death was unreasonable, and so are the forms of consolation.

Many months later, I was re-reading his works, in order to write a critical essay to accompany *The Hill Station*, in the volume edited by Jim's close friend John Spurling. I was thinking of the past, and also of Olivia; at the back of my mind, as I wrote my first impersonal paragraphs about J. G. Farrell's prose style, was the dim feeling that that evening I was going to see Olivia, and that we would talk about Jim. I closed my typewriter, and as I did so recalled that I was not going to see Olivia at all, for Olivia too was by then dead. I was, in fact, going to a meeting in Olivia's memory at the PEN Club. But what remained with me was not so much shock and sadness as the comforting knowledge that we had all indeed been friends, and that our friendship was part of a wider network in time and out of time. Some of his friends became mine; some of mine became his. There is a continuity. And the memories are good.

Gimpel the Fool

D. J. ENRIGHT

'There even Gimpel cannot be deceived' –
Which is a beginning. Though only a start.
As well as truly, he should be well received.
I wish for him a virgin. There are surely
Such in heaven. (No giving in marriage there.)
I wish him marriage too. All things may be.

And for one who is not exactly bright
(Would we wish him light perpetual?)
Shades of science, flavours of philosophy,
Are neither here nor there. (And even passé.)
What is proposed is what is known as happiness,
For a moderate man a little largesse,
But shatter-proof and plentiful.

Long deceived, one deserves to be undeceived
For longer. Moderation beyond all measure,
Marriage (with a virgin) and plain honest pleasure.
Every story paints a picture of some truth,
Whatever is envisaged must exist, if only there –
There is no deceiving Gimpel in the future.

Jessica

SUSAN HILL

Expectant mothers rarely admit openly to wanting either a son or a daughter. You dare not; it would be tempting fate. 'Which are you hoping for?' they ask. There is an absolutely standard reply. 'We don't mind, so long as it's all right.' And indeed, oh indeed, that is the truth. And yet . . .

All the time I was carrying her, I thought of her, in my conscious mind, as 'he'. *Did* I want a son? I would never have said so. 'So long as it's all right . . .'

But I did. Not because I prefer boys; certainly not for any silly misplaced, dynastic reasons – we have no title, no great house, no vasty estates, no family firm, no ancient name. No. It was because I did not think I could cope with the mother-daughter relationship all over again, but from the other side, as it were. I made the mistake – I couldn't help but make it, then – of assuming that the relationship would somehow be a repeat performance, the same relationship as the one I had with my own mother. That was a difficult one. She was thirty-five when I was born. I was going to be thirty-five too. Superstitiously, I believed all the other similarities would hold.

One of the astonishingly, blindingly obvious, beautifully simple truths I have discovered since her birth is that, *of course* the relationship is not the same and never could have been so. I am me, I am not my mother; I am not even like her. And my daughter is utterly herself and is not me. And . . . oh, times have changed, and my life is a different kind of life, and my marriage is quite a different sort of marriage and so much else besides.

Nevertheless, I felt I would be safer with a son, history would not appear to be repeating itself. And a son would not – would he? – be too like me, just because he would *be* 'he'. I did not much want a chip off the old block.

My husband was much less devious, much more open about it, with himself and with the world. 'I want a little girl,' he would say, putting all his cards on the table, as he always does, leaving himself so vulnerable, so open to public disappointment, in a way I never could.

But I – sometimes, secretly and to myself alone, *I* would admit that I wanted a boy. And at the very same time, in my heart I knew, even as I wanted, that I would not have, I knew for certain that she was she.

So that, when she was born, in the early hours of a wet summer's morning, when she was held up, puce and slimy and screaming, a daughter for all the world to see, I felt no surprise, none. Relief, of course, of all sorts; relief to have been cast up on the beach at last after hours of being in the eye of the storm; relief that she was, indeed, 'all right'. And joy at seeing her father's joy, as he held the girl he wanted. But no surprise.

Then they gave her to me. Still puce, with a head moulded into a strange, martian shape by the forceps, the slime drying to white scales. For a second, she drew breath. The screaming stopped. She and I looked at one another. I felt not pleasure, not joy, not the uprush of love. Nothing other than recognition. I thought, but I *know you*, somehow, I have always known you. And I saw the recognition in her own eye gleam briefly back. So here we are, I thought then. Here, after all, she is. Of course.

You may know all there is to know about babies, children, but until your own is born, in a sense, you know nothing. People tell you, but you cannot take it in.

I had not known, could not have believed or understood, how completely and entirely *there* they are, from the moment they arrive, how utterly and altogether themselves, as they will be until the day they die, knowable, visible. At the age of half an hour, they show you exactly the kind of person they are. She did.

They took her away for the rest of the night, so that I could sleep and she could be under observation (because of the forceps). As I was being wheeled back into my room, at two o'clock in the morning, a nurse loomed over the side of the trolley. Young, red-haired. Irish. I can see her face if I close my eyes now, hear her soft voice. 'Now is it *your* baby I've just been bathing and giving a drink of water? Sure, she's a fine one! Only an hour old and looking all round, taking everything in with her big eyes, and shouldn't she be fast asleep?'

The next morning, they brought her in. She lay, looking out through the perspex sides of her cot, which reminded me of a plant propagator. Taking everything in. Great big eyes. Trying to make out this world.

'She's supposed to be asleep, and look at her. She's been like it since dawn. Doesn't want to miss a trick.' I picked her up. Our eyes met again.

She never did sleep much. At ten days old, she was being taken round her father's study and shown the collection of beautiful watercolours, while I slept. The health visitor called in when she was three weeks old. 'That baby is *focussing*.'

And so, for five and a half years now, it has been. Looking at everything. Not missing a trick. Taking it all in. Curious, enquiring, interested. Nosy. Alert.

I had never expected to have a child, not really. Perhaps no one does, perhaps we none of us believe we possibly could; even though through pregnancy and labour, in the teeth of all the evidence, there is a curious sense of disbelief and unreality, until that moment of coming face to face. But what I never consciously expected was the way she would change me. She herself, with her own personality, not just she, a child. Oh, of course it all comes as a shock, the way your entire life and household are turned on their heads, the way looking after a baby completely dominates your days and nights, intrudes and penetrates, like a sort of seeping, ever-expanding gas, into every crevice of your home, your daily existence, your awareness, your dreams.

That is not what I mean. I mean that *she* has changed me. I watch her, listen to her, learn from her, despair over her, am amazed by her. She is so totally herself, and so all-together. And so very separate from me. I can stand back from her and see what she is like, and that surprises me. The world is different to me now, too. I feel I have passed through a secret door, to which I was given the key at her birth. On the other side of it are people, emotions, experiences, knowledge, I did not know existed.

Her arrival and her presence make me part of a great solidarity of other mothers; I feel closer, in a curiously physical sense, to them. I used to feel a natural, rational, intellectual sense of horror and outrage at the world's sufferings. Since her birth I feel an emotional reaction to them that makes me weep easily, or sick in my stomach, or rage with the sort of rage that makes me cry out loud. She accentuates these emotions partly because she herself has a tender heart. She is a very loving, kind, concerned child, she would rescue a snail from the rain; she wants to be told, and to understand, about refugees and the underfed and the orphans and the deaf and the dumb and the blind, and to make it all better. She asks why. She gives God a hard time of it.

She is fiercely independent. 'I can do it by *myself*.' She has a sudden desire for privacy. 'Jessica's room. Privit.' The fury with me, for attempting to restrain, forbid, protect, sometimes even for knowing, being older, being me, boils up and overflows. We clash. 'An emotional couple,' a friend said. We shout and cry and resent and infuriate. And fall into each other's arms.

She is, at the moment, an only child. So was I. She has 'older' parents. So did I. I spent hours alone, most happily alone, playing with toys, playing imaginary games with imaginary companions. She does not, cannot. She has no real idea how to play with toys at all, and though her imagination is vivid, it is nurtured in company, preferably mine. That baffles me, and infuriates me, too. I would have given – still would – my eye teeth for a lot of solitude to get on with my own forms of play. But she is she, and I am I, and she will do fine, I know, so long as I remember that.

She is more sociable than I ever was, or am; she likes nothing more than a friend, and then, with a like-minded companion, she takes off into flights of imaginative play that I could never have dreamed of sharing. I admire that. Envy it.

I enjoy watching her be so confident, so outgoing, launching herself into the world, eyes wide open, taking it all in, and drawing anyone, everyone, into her circle. It is a great gift; she will never, I think, be lonely or embittered or dangerously introspective or self-pitying or seriously depressive, while she has it and uses it. I bless her most, perhaps, for being able so freely to go out from me, for never having been attached to the apron strings. I would have found a clinging child hard to bear. Yet she is warm and affectionate, too, a kisser, a hugger of a child, and that I bless, too, for my relationship with my own mother lacked that above all; she found it all impossible, poor woman, and so, with her, did I. But my own daughter distributes her loving favours generously, warmly, happily. Perhaps I should worry about that, as she grows up, but somehow I doubt if I will.

In many respects, she is utterly like a thousand other small children; she is insanely fussy, and touchy, and nervous of the dark and the witches and she looks like a dozen others, too, sturdy and open-round-faced, with unremarkably straight brown hair, neither pretty nor plain.

She is funny, with a strong, if erratic sense of her own funniness. Her vocabulary is wide, sensitive, precise, she reads easily and well, she has no ball sense, not much ability to run gracefully, a good musical ear, no talent for drawing. She is hurt easily, forgives easily, befriends easily. She is more than a little bossy. The mixture, as always, is unique.

Having her made me come to terms with myself once and for all.

It rooted and settled me. She has made me look at the world differently, fear less for myself and more for her, forgive the past, let the unimportant go. Her birth has liberated me. That July night, at the moment I first and finally met her, I grew up.

She will do the same.

A Romance in E Flat Minor

MICHAEL HOLROYD

When Rupert Brooke went to Rugby in the early 1900s, he noticed that a girl about half-a-dozen years older than himself would sometimes come and join the boys at meals. Her name was Erica Cotterill and she occupied a special place at Rugby, her aunt having married William Parker Brooke, Rupert's father and the house-master of School Field.

Erica was not popular with the boys. She had a habit of telling Mr Brooke which of them had taken 'too much pudding'. She was not a shy girl: rather someone who provoked shyness in others. But Rupert got on well with her and by 1904 the two of them had started a correspondence in which he took on the pose of a disillusioned decadent, and she volunteered to have wrung from her 'wonderful secrets' involving the possibility of duels between foreign gentlemen.

From his role as a nineties Bohemian Brooke was largely converted by the plays of Bernard Shaw on which he would drop in during flying visits to the Court Theatre in Sloane Square. 'My present pose is as a Socialist,' he concluded. In 1905 he had seen *Major Barbara*, 'a brutal sordid play, difficult to understand and very interesting', he told Erica. '. . . One of the characters utters a scathing invective against public school masters at which I applauded very suddenly and loudly in the midst of dead silence.' Even better was *John Bull's Other Island*. 'It is unspeakably delightful . . . exquisite, wonderful, terrific, an unapproachable satire on everything.'

It was while listening to this play in the autumn of 1905 that Erica suddenly felt herself overcome with Shaw's ejaculation of words. Having conceived this new literary enthusiasm, she poured out her passion in a letter to Shaw, signing herself 'Miss Charmer'. Following twenty years of neglect in Ireland and another twenty years of rejection in England, Shaw had been left with a need for attention: any kind of attention, even attention he desperately didn't want. So now, despite not knowing his correspondent's name and having no address other than 'Poste Restante, Godalming', he couldn't help replying. He told her that her romantic notions were the 'greatest nonsense' and that love was an infinite mystery 'like everything else, until you have been through it, when it becomes as finite as anything else'. He also recommended her to 'marry and have children: then you will not ask from works of art what you can get only from life'.

The effect of this letter was decisive, and Erica immediately transferred her infatuation from the plays to the playwright. She was twenty-four; he nearly fifty: and over the next dozen years she aimed at him erratic bursts of unpunctuated strangely compelling letters. 'So,' Shaw explained, 'I started giving her a little advice.' He advised her to join a socialist society ('there are always envelopes to be directed and tracts to be distributed'); and he advised her to 'get some business to do that is specially your own business'; otherwise (he advised her) she would go 'quite cracked'.

From her other literary mentor, Rupert Brooke, Erica had simultaneously switched on a parallel current of advice. '. . . For God's sake let me advise you,' he appealed. 'I'm glad you've been among people who live for Art. It must be very good for you. I love Art myself; especially in the evenings. But why are you not a Fabian? Which kind of non-Fabian are you? The feeble-minded, or the emotional.'

By provenance it was Erica (not Brooke) who should have been a Fabian. Her father, Charles Clement Cotterill, was an outspoken schoolmaster and socialist. He had signalled his revolutionary stance by refusing to wear a beard and by producing such books as (ambiance Brooke) *Suggested Reforms in Public Schools* and (ambiance Shaw) *Human Justice for Those at the Bottom*. Erica attempted to join literary ambition to Fabian interests by publishing a play called *A Professional Socialist*. She arrived with a copy of the play at Shaw's house. He nervously handed it to his wife who, while agreeing that it was 'remarkable', advised Erica to 'cut it'. In this play the character of Ursula Windridge straightforwardly states Erica's own quest:

'I want to find *real* passion . . . I want great blazing racing feelings that flame round you like a glorious wind; I want some gorgeous thing to live for with every atom of my own soul.'

That was certainly what Erica wanted: and her 'gorgeous thing' was G.B.S. She was full of intoxicated romance – something that Brooke, with his tidy rhymes, was understood to celebrate and that Shaw believed he had been sent into the world to trample on with thick boots. Erica provides an ironic commentary to both their careers, exposing the vacuity of Brooke's early poetic fancies and the inability of Shaw to enact his own ideas. Like a searchlight, she glances into their worlds, lighting up the respectability of the Bohemian and the timidity of the revolutionary. Erica feels, thinks, lives through the page as if it were her body; her writing is an orgasm of emotional experience. By contrast, the professional poet and professional dramatist appear to pluck their material from its natural ground, remove it indoors and press it on to paper. Shaw did this with Erica herself, adapting her first pseudonymous approach to him for use in his play *Getting Married*. When this disquisitory drama opened to a hail of critical denunciation at the Haymarket on 12 May 1908, Erica asked Brooke to the opening night and after a palpitating pause, he accepted her 'alluring' invitation. 'You are strangely practical,' he hazarded. '. . . I shall come. (Mother will swoon if she hears.) Only you are to behave and *not* "clutch my arm at thrilling moments" . . . Bring an umbrella & clutch that, if you must clutch . . . you must be very good & patient, & only speak when you explain the jokes to me.'

But *Getting Married* was more than a volley of jokes: it appeared to set forth all the dangers, injustices, anomalies in the institution of marriage; demonstrating that sex was the most gloriously impersonal part of human relations, and asserting the right of women to bear children without bearing the additional burden of a husband. Since Shaw had already advised Erica to have children, to experiment in life rather than in art, the lesson of the play was obvious. She would have *his* children – with Rupert Brooke as their godfather – and she dashed off a note to Shaw to advise him of this. His response disappointed her. 'Now it is clear that you can't marry me, because I am married already, and too old anyhow,' he argued.

'But please do not suppose that your loving me is the smallest reason for you not marrying someone else. On the contrary, it is an additional reason for doing it as soon as you can. To begin with, a great deal of *pain* in youthful love is purely physical. Every complete and vital person wants to fulfil the sexual function . . . and one will do as well as another for purposes of physical fulfilment.'

What seemed curious to Erica was that the author of *Getting Married* should use the word marriage as a synonym for sexual intercourse. To ensure that he did not misunderstand her she wrote again, and then again, until Shaw's advice grew more peremptory. 'Why not,' he urged, 'marry somebody with a short temper and a heavy fist, who will knock you down?' She must, he repeated, occupy herself with work and babies. Without these she would be 'a nagging prig'.

There was something about the way in which Erica accepted his advice that unnerved Shaw. Believing it was time her parents took some notice, he demanded that she make her love known and she agreed by threatening to write to H. G. Wells about it. In fact she seems to have confided her wonderful secret only to Rupert Brooke. 'I grieve for your nerves,' he responded, but cautiously restricted his Shavian references to literature, singling out as 'the best play in the world' *Candida* in which the youthful poet renounces domestic love (with a wife and children) for the solitude of literary inspiration.

Some of Erica's difficulties, Brooke diagnosed, came from her style (likened by Shaw to Dora Copperfield's) which, though it rose and fell with unflagging conviction, impressed him as being bewilderingly incoherent. She did everything too hurriedly. She should have cultivated some Fabian gradualism. 'The great thing is to *make other people understand what one means*,' Brooke hinted. 'So merely to blurt it out and understand it oneself, does not do . . .

'I think it is good to shock people a little, & speak out to them, but one must be careful to do it gradually, as a rule, so as to get them accustomed by degrees. Only, I think, if one really feels "inspired" – feels it *absolutely necessary* to tell out some burning thing – if one is sure of this feeling, to speak out is right at all costs. It is a matter to settle with one's own conscience, I think.'

This was how Erica did feel. Her conscience left her untroubled since her normal condition was one of 'inspiration' and she felt full of the necessity to speak out her burning love for Shaw. He had calculated that she was one third mad and always therefore on the verge of rousing his hatred for mad people who, nevertheless, he seemed increasingly to attract. Her letters bored him terribly yet their power was undeniable and though he longed to fling them into the waste paper basket, he often found himself glancing at them, beginning to read them, then actually replying, using the force of his own style to combat hers. He told her she was a 'luxurious young devil, with the ethics, and something of the figure, of an anteater'; that if she dared try crawl over him as she doubtless had crawled over Rupert Brooke, she would be 'hurled into outer darkness'; that whenever he received anything in the nature of a loveletter, he handed it straight to his wife.

Erica's reaction to this was to make her letters more easily available to Charlotte Shaw. Shaw himself had told her to type them, and to make her love public: so, in 1908 and 1909, using a printer in Sydney Street, Chelsea, she privately published her correspondence to Shaw. To this first series of about sixty thousand words she subsequently added during the First World War (after Rupert Brooke had died and his restraining influence been removed) another two hundred thousand printed words entitled 'An account' or 'An account through Letters' which she dedicated to Shaw 'whom I love': over a quarter-of-a-million words of self-indulgent, oddly eloquent stream-of-consciousness prose.

'I am conscious from the beginning of writing this to you that it will be printed, but yet everything I write I shall write to you alone, and in the same way as Ive written to you before, out of a feeling that I am speaking to you, more than I am writing to you. You know how Ive written, over and over in different forms, that it felt that so long as I consciously held back from giving one thing that I could give for this thing which is my love for you that I should be held back from everything, and you know how nearly from the beginning a thing has come back and back in me, a feeling that I needed to go, and kneel down to you in front of people . . . I spread things out through writing, I didn't hide them, nor the form they came in, and I kneeled down to you before people in my imagination, but held back from kneeling down to you with my body – '

It is from her imagination that she writes. She is obsessional, relentless, ecstatic, insistent: and as unstoppable in her fashion as Shaw himself. She repeats and repeats. Her prose is hypnotic, like a chant, a litany, ascending in exaltation, curling about itself monotonously and sinking so it may rise again and then again, again. The ritual of this writing was the vehicle for her love, fuelled by religious fantasies of sex: of conception and birth. She summons Shaw to look round and confront all he had deliberately turned his back on.

'. . . What is coming is coming my dear hearts stretch out to meet what comes out of some part in you which is deeper than what you mostly stretch out of to meet things which come through words . . . can you feel a dim dim knowledge in you that behind a single separate thing are things which are struggling to push out through you – and will you pray for me my dear ones not only out of dim feelings in you but still more out of everything that laughs and dances in you – its as if if inside you you

stretched out your hands and took my hands out of everything that laughs
and dances in you I should reach my love.'

Shaw's weapon against passion was iron politeness. He was
magnificently armed with good manners, jokes, witty advice,
reverberating words: and he banged them all off at her. But she had
as many words in her armoury as he did and used a different
vocabulary. Her talent was 'as irresistible as Shelley's & Tolstoy's
rolled into one' and she would 'either die a lunatic before you are
33', he prophesied, 'or be the greatest English woman writer –
indeed one of the greatest of English writers – before you are 40'.
This tribute Erica sensibly preserved and had printed almost thirty
years later wrapped round her anonymous novel *Form of Diary*
(Pushkin Press, 1939).

In fulfilling neither of Shaw's prophecies exactly, Erica lived what
by Shavian standards was a lunatic existence until her seventieth
year. How strange were women! Shaw had taken the trouble to give
her notice of his Fabian lectures, send her theatre tickets, introduce
her to friends, demand information about her home, inform her
about publishing contracts and promise to 'exude wisdom at every
pore': and still she did not feel discouraged. Charlotte, his wife,
actually accused him of encouraging the girl. Extraordinary! Was it
his fault if she camped in the woods nearby or rented the
neighbouring cottage or came racing up to his house on a
motorbicycle under the trance-like impression that it belonged to
her? Finally they were forced to threaten her with the police. 'I
would not stand it from Cleopatra herself,' cried Shaw, who drafted
a stern letter for his wife to write which explained that he 'is quite
friendly and sympathetic with everybody, from dogs & cats to
dukes & duchesses; and none of them can imagine that his universal
friendliness is not a special regard for them. He has already allowed
you to become far more attracted to him than he should; and I do
not intend to let you drift any further into an impossible position.'

Yet behind the boredom and impossibility of it all, there was
some 'special regard' between them. Erica's account of their

relationship, though choked with her own symptoms, has clear insights into his nature and, when it touches on fact, is accurate, comparing closely with his correspondence. 'One day when I was in a train with you,' she writes, 'you suddenly leaned forward and said – Now Ill tell you what Id tell few women, you told it and I answered you and presently you said – Ill leave the country.' Shaw's version of this episode is perhaps used in Act 2 of *Heartbreak House* where Captain Shotover (Shaw) and Ellie Dunn (Erica) go to the sofa and talk.

CAPTAIN SHOTOVER. What did you expect? A Saviour, eh? Are you old-fashioned enough to believe in that?

ELLIE. No. But I thought you were very wise, and might help me. Now I have found you out. You pretend to be busy, and think of five things to say and run in and out to surprise people by saying them, and get away before they can answer you.

CAPTAIN SHOTOVER. It confuses me to be answered. It discourages me. I cannot bear men and women. I have to run away. I must run away now *he tries to*

ELLIE. (*again seizing his arm*). You shall not run away from me. I can hypnotize you. You are the only person in the house I can say what I like to. I know you are fond of me. Sit down. (*She draws him to the sofa*) . . .

ELLIE. . . . Dream. I like you to dream. You must never be in the real world when we talk together.

CAPTAIN SHOTOVER. I am too weary to resist or too weak. I am in my second childhood. I do not see you as you really are. I cant remember what I really am. I feel nothing but the accursed happiness I have dreaded all my life long: the happiness that comes as life goes, the happiness of yielding and dreaming instead of resisting and doing, the sweetness of the fruit that is going rotten.

ELLIE. You dread it almost as much as I used to dread losing my dreams and having to fight and do things. But that is all over for me: my dreams are dashed to pieces. I should like to marry a very old, very rich man. I should like to marry you.

Erica lived in 'a fanciful world of her own', Shaw wrote; and in the fanciful world of his plays she has a special place for she was, he acknowledged, 'an exquisite sort of person'. But in the world of facts and actions they were severely incompatible. When over fifty she adopted two baby boys whom she was reputed to feed largely on peanut butter. She changed her name to Mrs. Saye and gave that name to the children whom she brought up as farmers in North Devon. But nothing went the way of her dreams — one of the boys forged her signature on a cheque and ran off with a married woman much older than himself whom Erica had thought of as her friend.

She died in 1950, the same year as Shaw himself. 'What a relief!' he exclaimed when he heard the news. She had been a terror and a nuisance and he had never wholly got over his dread that she might roar up on her motorbicycle again one night. Yet he would have been happy to see her on what he called 'reasonable terms' — that is, pressed on to paper as an ingredient for his fantasy. So now that she was safely dead, he wrote to ask a friend: 'Are any photographs of her obtainable?'

Sketching a Thatcher

TED HUGHES

Bird-bones is on the roof. Seventy eight
And still a ladder-squirrel,
Three or four nitches at a time, up forty rungs,
Then crabbing out across the traverse,
Cackling his gristly merriment,
Cock-crows of insulting banter, liberated
Into his old age, like a royal fool,
But still tortured with energy. Thatching
Must be a sinless job. Weathered
Like a weathercock, face bright as a ploughshare,
Skinny forearms of steely cable, batting
The reeds flush, crawling, cliff-hanging,
Lizard-silk of his skinny lizard-skinny hands,
Hands never still, twist of body never still –
Bounds in for a cup of tea, 'Caught you all asleep!'
Markets all the gossip, all the bad-mouthing
His sons have netted, and the wives of his sons,
Pries out every possibility – cynical old goblin,
Crowing with wicked joy. Bounds out –
Trips and goes full length, bounces back upright,
'Haven't got the weight to get hurt with!' Cheers
Every departure – 'Off for a drink?' and 'Off
To see his fancy woman again!', leans from the sky,
Sun-burned-out pale eyes, eyes bleached
As old thatch, in the worn tool of his face,
A machine of mechanical merriment, hacking its iron,
In his haggard pants and his tired-out shirt –
They can't keep up with him. He just can't

Stop working. 'I don't want the money!' He'd
Prefer a few years. 'Have to sell the house to pay me!'
Lean, quick face from the undergrowth, elvish warrior,
Alertness built into its weasel bone,
Quickness into the bird-bright sharpness
And hook of his nose, bill-hook of his face.
Suns have worn him, like an old sun-tool
Of the day-making, an old shoe-tongue
Of the travelling weathers, the hand-palm, ageless,
Of all winds on all roofs. He lams the roof
And the house quakes. Was everybody
Once like him? He's squirmed through
Some tight cranny of natural selection
With a hawk-fling of wild spirit.
Merry as a mink. Biologically merry.
The nut-stick yealm-twist's got into his soul,
He didn't break. He's proof
As his crusty roofs. And too quick-vertical
For spirit-sludge to collect and thicken in him
To puddling malaise. He ladder-dances
His blood light as spirit. His muscles
Must be clean as horn. And the whole house
Is more pleased with itself, him on it,
Cresting it, and grooming it, and slapping it
Than if an eagle rested there. Sitting,
Drinking his tea, he looks like a tatty old eagle
And his yelping laugh of derision
Is just like a tatty old eagle's.

John Stewart Collis

RICHARD INGRAMS

I am a book snob in the way other people are wine or people snobs. I have never been able to read a book that is not well written. There has to be an element, if not of humour, then of what Johnson called 'wit'. Dismissing a play by a contemporary he said, 'It has not wit enough to keep it sweet', going on to translate 'wit' as 'vitality'. Wit is a better word because it suggests a humorous spirit – something that keeps writing alive; but it may also involve prejudice – strong personal feelings of the sort that make writers like Cobbett or Orwell so readable, even though most of the things they wrote about have long since been forgotten.

Ever on the look-out for writing, new or old, which has this elusive and enduring quality of 'wit' I was interested when in 1972 I first heard the name of John Stewart Collis mentioned by Dick Merricks, a farmer in Sussex, one of whose sons had been a patient of Collis's physiotherapist wife. I gathered from Merricks that Collis had written a lot about natural phenomena as well as some books about farming life. Some time later I came across a copy of *While Following the Plough*, published by Jonathan Cape in 1946 with wood engravings by Barbara Allen, which I bought for 50p. After a few pages I knew it was a find. The book describes in a series of short sequences the author's life as a farm labourer in Sussex and in Dorset during the war. Unlike most books of this sort, it is neither sentimental nor nostalgic. Collis describes in a very detailed way exactly what farm work involves and his own clumsy efforts to carry out the day-to-day tasks. He tells you about his fellow workers, notably about his boss – surely one of the best portraits ever of a farmer:

'A farmer is called by his men either "the boss" or "the guvnor" or "the master" (now out of date), or "the old man" (regardless of age), or more often simply "he". He is never called "the chief".

'At this farm he was sometimes called "the boss", often enough "the old man", generally "He", or, more properly, "'E", and sometimes merely "the van". He used a second-hand butcher's van for getting about the premises and carrying oil and what not from one scene of operation to another. So one would hear – "Look out, there's the van!" or "I didn't see no van" when his whereabouts was doubtful. But on the whole he was designated simply as "'E" – "'E's coming!" . . .

'He was a man somewhere in his fifties. His eyes were impressive in their mildness, but his mouth was large and ugly, partly concealed by a stumpy moustache. You could recognize him a long way off by his walk. He took huge strides, head bent slightly down, like a man measuring a cricket pitch. That walk was very characteristic. There was no dawdling nor diddling about him: he never strolled; he never looked quietly at the scene; he never took out a pipe nor smoked a cigarette, any more than he would be likely to drink a glass of beer, pat a dog, or say good night, good morning, or thank you. He was on the go the whole time, as if his life depended on it . . .'

Throughout *While Following the Plough* there are plenty of digressions, mainly about literature. But the main point of the book is its vivid account of Collis's own discovery in his humdrum tasks of the sense of wonder at the extraordinary nature of the creation. I finished it with intense enjoyment and since then have read its sequel *Down to Earth*, much of which is concerned with trees, and almost all of Collis's other books, including his biographies of Tolstoy, Strindberg, Columbus and Carlyle.

Some time after writing a review of *Living with a Stranger* in the *Spectator* in 1978 I heard from Collis himself. 'Have you ever an idle hour, a quarter hour really to spend at 11 p.m. of an evening?' he asked. 'The BBC, Radio 4, Book at Bedtime, are broadcasting extracts from *The Worm Forgives the Plough* – the two farming books in one volume – from January 26 (next Monday) to February 6th.' Naturally I made a point of listening. The reader was Alan Badel, an excellent choice. Having himself been an RAF pilot in the

Normandy landings, it was fitting that he should end the readings
with this passage: 'In the day of calamity, in the day of battle, all
men must cease from work and rise to slay. All save the ploughman.
He must go on. Hence the gesture of that immortal ploughman on
the fields of Normandy. When D. Day came and battle raged upon
the beaches; when the sky was filled with fighters and the land was
lashed with fire, that nameless Man took out his plough and did his
work and turned his furrow in the midst of all! And when the brief
hurricane of mortal men had passed, he was still there.' I remember
lying in bed thinking, 'Yes, that is the real thing', and experiencing
the sense of excitement you get from being in close touch with
genius.

It was some weeks later that my wife and I invited ourselves to
call on Collis at his house in Surrey woodland near Dorking. I had
imagined, I think, a more austere and dignified figure than the
ruddy, twinkling Irishman who almost bounded out to greet us.
One expects men of genius to be solemn and serious, but in my
limited experience they are laughing and humorous. (At first sight
the famous portrait of Bach makes him seem a stern figure; but if
you look closely you will see that he is smiling.) It was certainly hard
to accept that here was a man of eighty. You couldn't think of him
in a conventional way as an old man for whom allowances must be
made.

On that occasion, as we sat in his pleasant sitting room after
lunch, Collis told me some of the circumstances of his life: 'For me it
was a case of life begins at seventy,' he said. 'I feel I have been
accepted by posterity without first being required to die.' *While
Following the Plough*, the book I admired so much, had been
rejected by twelve publishers before Cape's finally accepted it. Even
then – incredibly – their reader Daniel George had found fault with
the writing and insisted on changes being made. (Collis, after a
suitable interval, returned the MS politely saying that having taken
advantage of their kind criticisms, he had made substantial
amendments. Actually he had not altered a single sentence. They

expressed themselves delighted with the improvements.) During the fifties he had written a number of what he calls his 'phenomenon' books – *Paths of Light, The Triumph of the Tree, The Moving Waters* – but though they were favourably reviewed they did not sell. Collis became well known in literary circles as a 'neglected' writer, a lethal word which he began to dread when applied to himself – 'If people think you're neglected they say "Very well, let's neglect him some more."' Much of his time during the sixties was taken up with nursing his invalid wife. Meanwhile, he says, 'I was more or less invisible.' But although very poor, Collis never became embittered – 'I certainly found it a long haul. I always thought this book (just done) will bring my ship home. But it never did. I possess very little courage, physically, mentally or morally. But I have had the courage to grapple with the publisher's rejection slip, or, in my own case, letter. I would open the letter and instantly turn to the last paragraph, the concluding words. I would look for them with lightning speed, and after I had seen the words " will return your MS under separate cover" would then start at the beginning. But the traumatic effect did not last longer than midday when with a feeling akin to exhilaration, I determined to soldier on, saying to myself, heaven knows why! – "My time is not yet, but my time will come."'

That time came at last when at the age of seventy, shortly after the death of his wife, Collis wrote his memoirs *Bound Upon a Course*. With his usual directness he looked back over his life. He tells of his childhood as the son of an Irish solicitor and one of a pair of twins, whose mother, as apparently sometimes happens with twins, worshipped his brother and hated him. The experience probably helped to shape his sense of humour and detachment, enabling him later to bear neglect of another kind. Collis went to Rugby and Oxford and before his crucial decision in 1940 to become a farm worker spent many years on the fringes of literary life in London, researching in the British Museum Reading Room, writing what he calls 'good-bad' books and meeting friends like Stephen Potter, also at that time a struggling would-be literary man, and G. B. Edwards, whose masterpiece, *The Book of Ebenezer le Page*, was only published long after his death.

His autobiography finished, Collis once again found it hard to get a publisher but eventually the book was accepted by Sidgwick and Jackson. It was extraordinarily well-received by critics and paved the way to a Collis revival. A publisher brought out *The Vision of Glory* which included most of *The Triumph of the Tree*, *The Moving Waters* and *Paths of Light*. When thus compressed into one volume it was clear what Collis had actually achieved in making a synthesis of science and poetry; and the book received great acclaim. This led to the publication of *While Following the Plough* and *Down to Earth* in one volume under the title of *The Worm Forgives the Plough*. This in turn led to Penguin publication of both books, and also to a TV dramatization of *The Worm*. Thus Collis began to enjoy the recognition that had eluded him all his life – 'and at a time when I should have been on the way out'.

In 1974 Collis had another stroke of good fortune when he married Irene, the widow of Sir Edward Beddington-Behrens, a remarkable and very talented person – a singer, a painter, a linguist (she was the first translator of Françoise Sagan and other French writers). Living in a well-ordered house at Abinger Common looking out over paddocks, grazing cows and tall pine trees, Collis for the first time in his life can write at leisure and take his time over book reviews – a job which most people think of as hack-work but which he treats as an art-form, bringing to it all the vitality of a man of thirty. In the last few years he has had great pleasure in contributing to the *Spectator*.

Revisiting Park House in November 1982 I asked Collis what writing involves for him. For a start, although he is tremendously painstaking and proudly informs me how he once rang the *Spectator* to ask them to change a comma in one of his reviews, he won't hear a word about 'discipline'. 'You can hear an author tell you how he works so many hours in the morning, then he has lunch, then he takes the dog for a walk, then so many hours more writing –

with me it's a complete shambles! I may spend half the morning looking for some reference which I have lost and then go off to play tennis if I feel like it.' He sets great store by technique but thinks of technique as inspirational. The beginning of a book, or even a book review is very important – 'finding a way in'. But how it happens can only be explained in terms of inspiration. People ask him about his quotations – gathered from so many unlikely sources – how did they come along? They seemed to come along very happily, is Collis's reply. As for his 'expositions', those passages where he explains complex scientific matters in simple terms, he says: 'I have never thought of it as a method – but simply as plain common sense to worry out *what has actually been said* by the experts and then "get it straight" as I would say to myself. I once found a quotation from *The Plough* in a book called *A Foundation Course in English* – a book with twenty-five chapters with examples taken from various luminaries. After the quote from my stuff there were headings such as "Expressive words and phrases" or "Giving a vivid impression" or "The expression of sounds" or about the writer's use of "echoing words" and what not; the student being supposed to analyse all this and note what adjectives could be used or should be left out. I found all this very curious – for to me it was entirely a matter of common sense.'

Collis himself is proudest of his 'phenomenon' books and especially of the fact that though he has written, as a layman, on complex scientific things he has never once been taken to task by a professional. Personally I think his greatest achievement is *The Worm Forgives the Plough*, not only because it has an abundance of 'wit', but because it is so many different things: a picture of farm life that has gone for ever; a picture of Collis's fellow workers; a picture of Collis himself struggling to come to terms with his unhelpful environment. (No book can be true to life which does not present life as a struggle.) All of this is interspersed with those moments of poetic insight which you get only from the true Romantic, the man, that is, who discerns the extraordinary in the ordinary. This is a book which I feel certain will live on when most of our contemporary nonsense has been forgotten. I had that certainty confirmed when, on the occasion of my November 1982 visit, Collis sat at his desk, his stockinged feet resting on a cushion, and read me in his soft Irish voice the following passage – and suddenly I felt very fortunate to be sitting there listening:

'We were now on a field beside that piece of kale I had first hoed, those plants that had seemed so poor in promise. The miserable stalks that I remembered were now as thick as a man's leg and as high as the waist or shoulders – and again I marvelled at the march. We worked very late that evening, and it was an especially lovely one. The wind had gone down completely and all the shapes of earth captured in the yellow rays were sculptured by their shades. The sun set and the dusk gathered, and with it came a deeper silence, as when a clock stops ticking in a silent room; the clouds had got stuck and would never move again; the new moon stooped down so low above a tree that I could have hung my hat upon its horn. The final tricky part of the rick making began when, the platform growing very narrow, I had to handle the sheaves with much circumspection. Down below I could see the roads becoming whiter and the fields darker and the woods more sombre, and as I glanced at them it occurred to me that perhaps after all this is how I would prefer to catch sight of Beauty – through the corner of my eye, while immersed in something else, while not seeking it at all.'

Is it Alas, Poor Yorick?

P. J. KAVANAGH

Recently I have started doing sums in my head: how old was my father when I was my sons' age, and how did he deal with me? I am always startled. What — that fifty-year-old figure of authority that I remember? (No, not authority but confidence, completedness, a man who had solved his problems and now stood on top of the hill looking calmly back and calmly on.) Am I really his age now, who am not like that at all, neither calm nor complete, and unlikely to be so?

I try to console myself with the thought that I probably appear to my sons as he did to me (though I doubt this) and tell myself, more confidently, that he was not really like that either.

I recently came across some early letters of his, written to his distant parents, explaining why he had given up his medical studies and had decided, against their wishes, to get married. I recognized the tone at once, slightly blustering, self-exculpatory; I had used to him. One of his excuses for his lack of industry is so far-fetched as to be possibly true. Overcome by thirst in the laboratory he had swigged a beaker of clear fluid which turned out to contain some deadly acid. This affected his work and, he tells them, permanently damaged his health. As he often boasted to me that he had never had a day's illness in his life, which in my experience was true, he had either conveniently forgotten this or, to his parents, was pulling the longbow as far as his bulging cheek would allow. But there is definitely a young man's rather whingeing note in the letter; slight, but sad. So when did he become the confident figure I remember? No, that's not right, he wasn't confident, he was diffident, but I derived confidence from him . . . So do I go on puzzling, nuzzling at his shade.

If you push into a thicket you sometimes come across a greening sheep-skull. Outside the thicket, plump, living sheep tear confidently at the grass, undismayed. We are like that, and should be. We miss our dead – sometimes we even grieve. It is hard to imagine that one day we will be among them. But meanwhile it is well to remember that through all sorts of cycles of change they nourish us, and continue to set us problems that will be with us until we die. So, having done my sums, I try to remember how he, fifty, dealt with me at fourteen – but I can't. Perhaps he didn't deal with me at all. But maybe it is not too late; he was, after all, a Roman Catholic, as in essence I am, so perhaps I should pray to him and ask his advice? But I can't do that either, can only imagine him embarrassed, evasive of my intensities, as he was in life; properly so as I now think. Thus he eludes me still, which is perhaps why I think of him so much.

But it is also because I feel myself in a special position because of him. He was not, I feel pig-headedly certain, like any other father. He didn't even *look* like any other father. He wore black, broad-brimmed hats for a start. Not very broad-brimmed, not sombreros, but not neat trilbys either. He was red-faced and red-haired, balding, with a huge dome, and was stout, to the extent of appearing almost square when I knew him, balanced on tiny feet. Someone painted a portrait of him and friends complained the painting made him look like a butcher. He could have looked like a butcher but he did not. Whether he was distinguished-looking I have no idea but he was certainly distinctive. I have never seen anyone who reminded me of him, even remotely. With his neat red moustache he might have been a bank manager, I suppose, or a retired army officer – but it would have been impossible to imagine which bank, or which army. A conundrum, you just could not place him; New Zealander-Irish he was as near as possible classless. When he briefly had a large desk in an office of his own making, even when he sat behind it, he gave the impression he was just passing through, was about to reach for his hat and go out into his beloved London – if indeed he wasn't already wearing the hat, which was usually the case.

He had no job, like other fathers, not a real one. He began adult life as a remittance man and when the remittances stopped he remained impoverished for a time, apparently not noticing. Then he suddenly began writing sketches for comedians and these, as the years passed, turned into radio shows which culminated in ITMA, the wartime programme that made him famous and, briefly, in funds; both of which he enjoyed. My point is this: he was, and is, my exemplar of order, an order I would like to pass on to my sons: but how can I when my own father spent his life, earned his living, presenting a sort of inspired, zany *dis*order as a source of true heart's ease? And every kind of authority as ludicrous? If he invented a mayor that mayor was amiably bent; if he wrote of a doctor that doctor was the source of every possible confusion to his patients. Each generation tries to be less pompous than its predecessor. I have watched my friends, the interesting ones, define themselves by reacting against their parents – against a too-limiting sense of class, or convention, or morality. (I have also sometimes seen them look aghast at the disordered world they have created, and attempt, too late, to swing back to the values of their parents.) But my father did not impose himself like that. Not that it was Liberty Hall. I once turned him purple with rage (an almost unique occurrence) because I used a fairly mild swear-word. But I can hardly define myself by going around cussing all the time.

His working methods were cottage-industry and bordered on the chaotic. He would leave it till the deadline and then get up in the middle of the night and sit at a tiny table in front of the electric fire, Parker pen in his stubby fingers, filling the ash-tray and sheets of lined foolscap which he dropped on the floor. By the time I surfaced he had covered the carpet with paper and was wandering in to the kitchen, reading bits out to my mother to see if she laughed, laughing himself anyway.

Of course it, and he, was not all good. That period of unemployed impoverishment showed irresponsibility – he had a family. Later he often drank too much – in company, never at home. Indeed I suspected that, among friends, he hardly noticed that he was drinking at all, just emptied what came to hand, as he had in the laboratory. In company the puns flowed easily, without malice. They no longer work, they were born of the moment, but I remember one occasion when a friend called Watt warned him about the excessive drinking of one of my father's business associates named Blatt: 'But surely,' said my father, 'that's a case of the Watt calling the kettle Blatt?' and what could have been an embarrassing, possibly unpleasant, moment went up in a shout of laughter. I remember admiring him for that, for the quickness of it, the geniality.

The image of the sheep-skull keeps returning to me . . . The most famous skull is Yorick's, and he was a jester too. I have sometimes suspected that Yorick is the secret hero of *Hamlet*. Certainly he is a hero of Hamlet's. Does he not, at the intensest moments of his confusion and grief, express himself in wild whirling word-plays?

My father didn't go in for giving advice (though he did once solemnly recommend that I keep a bottle of Vichy water by my bedside). He didn't himself – he drank enormous quantities of lime-juice instead and I certainly never saw him with a hangover however much he had deserved one – but he saw no self-contradiction in that. He told me that I should never go bald if I massaged my scalp in a certain way, as he always had. He placed his square finger-tips on his shining dome in order to show me how. However, when I was hit by a grief, he did venture an oblique suggestion during the course of a shy tête-à-tête lunch. 'Now that something terrible has happened to you,' he said, 'perhaps you'll write comedy.' Coming from him that is not quite the show must go on, laugh, clown, laugh cliché it might otherwise sound. For what was there in my father's life? There was God, there was fellowship, and there were jokes. It is not a bad recipe. At times I have detested jokes – a son must react against his father in some fashion. I have seen jokes for the evasions they are, what Edward Thomas called the 'monkey, humour' praising Richard Jefferies for his lack of it. If you sit in a room with a TV comedy going on next door and hear the automaton-like burst of hilarity it is possible to hate laughter itself.

But my pendulum swings. Sometimes I think jokes are the only truly serious response to our absurd fates. Who can match the desperate humourlessness of the adolescent who thinks he is the first to discover seriousness? (I was probably like that, which is why my father ducked.) For after all the show *must* go on. The alternative is not a joke.

Maybe what my father meant, but was too gentle to say, was that now something terrible had happened to me perhaps I might grow up. I would like to ask him about that now because I suspect he never quite did so himself and this has impeded my own growing-up, for which I bless him, however tiresome I may be to others. For I am never wholly at ease with those who have come too surely to terms with life. I would also like to ask Yorick, that fellow of infinite jest, what he would have said if he had heard Hamlet say 'Alas'. Something to the point, surely, but not portentous.

So I go on puzzling, nuzzling the green grass outside the thicket.

The Good and the Beautiful

MARGHANITA LASKI

What my first school fitted its pupils for was to be citizens of an utopia very like William Morris's Nowhere, only more liberal, less socialistic, and this not surprisingly since we children were led to believe (and possibly correctly) that the school had been founded by the famous Editor of the *Coketown Guardian* so that his own children should receive right education before, of course, the Coketown Grammar School for the boys, the Coketown High School for the girls. Within such limitations, what there could be of beauty and preparation for the ideal *polis*, that we had; and there was no one (I am still sure of this), no one then better to transmit the very spirit of the ideals than the woman I shall call Miss Anderson who had taken over the headmistress-ship just before I went there.

The murmurings that were heard, sometimes, about new brooms sweeping over-clean, as when, for example, the old woman who taught French ('Le drapeau anglais est rouge, blanc, et bleu') was dismissed, lead me now to suppose that when Miss Anderson took over, the school wasn't what it had been and that it was her business to make it so again; which she did. I don't suppose the structure was helpful. Memory faintly intimates a large Victorian gentleman's villa, but in those days, few people, and certainly not children, looked at architecture – those merry intellectuals of *The Weekend Book* never glanced at a building – though I do recall a school hall beautiful with green oak (yes, green oak) half-panelling. Beautiful is the word I most often want to use in recalling the more fragile moveables inside the school, and these, surely, were owed to Miss Anderson: beautiful the prints and rhyme-sheets on the walls, the home-made charts for the history lessons, less usual then, the *things* we made in Handicrafts – no child came out of that school unable to cane a basket, thong a leather bag, rush a chair, raffia a mat, twist a snaky pot and even mould one, and dovetail a wooden box, even if such bread-and-butter work as darning, and sewing seams was left to the home. Beautiful, too, were the clothes we wore, mauve shantung tunics for eurhythmics, and summer school tunics in sky-blue cotton, embroidered in free-expression flowers by such mothers as could. And most beautiful of all was Miss Anderson's study.

I don't suppose that Miss Anderson's pale grey walls and William-Morris linens were surprising to that substantial group of children whose parents worked at the University the far side of the main road. To me, they were a culture-shock of beauty in use, comparable only with the first time I was taken, in London, to see Heal's, and why this was so, is part of the story.

For I was a Jewish child, of a mother in every waking moment aware that she was an exile from London and that she was a Sephardi, which is a kind of very superior Jew of whom there are only a few, so superior that to mix with the other kind of Jews who are called Ashkenazis was almost as bad as mixing with the Goys, who are the rest of you. And the only other middle-class Sephardis in Coketown then with whom my mother could safely socialize, were an exotic group indeed, mostly very rich, often very beautiful people who came from around the Mediterranean, anywhere from Morocco to Turkey, with, most of them, French as their first language. They had come to Coketown through the cotton trade, but still in their homes, which were the only homes in Coketown I went into, they lived like Orientals, in their food, their furnishings, and their manners. Their end, in Coketown, which came with the slump, was tragic, but at the time I write of, all was very well with them, and of course, their children went to Miss Anderson's school. It was the best school.

Nowadays, both parents and teachers would be aware of the need to do, of something being done, about assimilation. Miss Anderson, in unassailable assurance of right standards, simply did it. I can't speak for other children, but by then I needed assimilation as much as any of them, and I know that one-third of all the culture that has since made life worthwhile to me came from her. Through her we learnt, in gross and in detail, that beauty and goodness were inextricably entwined, and the importance of being educated without marks or placings because these were competitive and ugly; although we did have end-of-term exams with marks, because this was, after all, Coketown, and one had to be realistic. We knew, as we all discovered at next school, a really unusual amount of all academic subjects, and we knew a great many plays too, some from performing them, like, unavoidably, Maeterlinck's *Blue Bird*, and some from reading only, like Marlowe's *Faustus*, for Miss Anderson never laid clumsy hands on what was best taken in alone. And through her I learned – we all learned – never to take the English language for granted. That I could already, at the age of seven, remember and know how to use such an expression as the one about new brooms sweeping clean was a measure of her success. Before we left, we all knew how to use those figures of speech omitted from the latest *Fowler*, like litotes and anacoluthon. We could parse and analyse any sentence in English, tell you the prosodic form of almost any verse, and we knew by heart enough Shakespeare and other poetry to see us, as it proved, through any air raid. Through a liberal education and a liberal use of the arts, I remember thinking as the bombs fell, Miss Anderson had given her pupils what would stand them in the best of steads in even the worst of times.

So we passed through and we left, I at thirteen to go to a school like a prison in London and never be happy again until I went to Somerville which had much the same attitudes as Miss Anderson's, or so it seemed to me then. And I remembered her with reverence and gratitude until it happened that I had to visit Coketown for two jobs of work with time to spare between them, and why not, as I said to my mother, no longer exiled from London, go and call on Miss Anderson?

But she, who in the old days had admired Miss Anderson as much as I did, was doubtful. She'd heard things, she said, and, What things? I demanded, but she didn't like to say, perhaps it was all untrue, maybe best if I went to see.

So when I went to Coketown, I telephoned and was asked to tea. The school had moved out to the suburbs now, but Miss Anderson's sitting-room seemed much as it was, a shrine (if now a rather faded shrine) of the very best ideals.

'You were one of the Jewish children, weren't you?' she began, as she poured the tea, and with it, hideously, hatred; the Jewish children, yes, she recalled them, always noisy, ostentatious, over-dressed, the mothers flamboyant, raucous, throwing their money around, the Jews vulgar, unassimilable, and Hitler, Hitler, had been right.

I was, I said, pressed for time, my taxi was waiting, mustn't go without saying how grateful I was for all she'd done for me. She wrote to me afterwards. She'd heard I was a writer, she said, and would I do a piece she could use in an appeal for the school? I refused and told her why. It was unthinkable not to tell her the truth.

I can find no ending that would not be intolerably moralistic. So I leave it at that.

Sir John Betjeman

ELIZABETH LONGFORD

My first memory of John is during a tête-à-tête lunch with Maurice Bowra, the celebrated wit and classical don, then Dean of Wadham College, Oxford. Suddenly there was a knock and a fawn-like head with mischievous, sparkling brown eyes peered round the door.

'Come in, then. You can get it. Help yourself,' bellowed Maurice. John darted into the bedroom and came out again with a dark suit over his arm. He was laughing uproariously. It was the first time I had heard that amazing laugh, which would certainly be called infectious and exhilarating and might also be thought wild, whooping and delirious; though none of those adjectives really conveys it. I can only suggest that anyone who made John laugh (and it wasn't difficult, for he loved it) thought they were hearing the first Paradisal green woodpecker 'yaffling' in the Tree of Knowledge.

After John had vanished, to my disappointment, I asked,

'Who is he? Why did he want your suit?'

'That's *Betjeman*.' Maurice always pronounced the name with great emphasis. 'He likes old things. He needs them. His father's rich.'

For several years afterwards I believed, erroneously, that John came from a stingy home and that Maurice clothed him out of pity. Today John can't remember why he borrowed the suit – perhaps for acting or a funeral – but says, 'I *do* like old things.'

The next time I met him was in the High, carrying a copy of the current number of the magazine *Cherwell*. He opened it at the page he himself had contributed: an ingenious sketch of two life-size shirt cuffs on which were printed all the answers a candidate could possibly need for the forthcoming divinity exam, known as

'Divvers'. By cutting along the dotted lines and pinning the paper cuffs over your own, you could not fail to pass. Alas, John failed 'Divvers' as often as the university regulations allowed him to take it, and he was duly sent down. It was some comfort to him that his examiner was Dr Wand who afterwards became Bishop of London. The irony was that this man who failed his religious test so often and so utterly, knew more about the churches than anyone else at Oxford, whether it was the high church St Paul's in Walton Street or Binsey to the west of Oxford, with St Margaret's well in its churchyard.

Meanwhile John had created for all of us a world of hilarious fantasy, in which real dons and undergraduates had been put through the sieve of his imagination and shaken out as gold and diamonds. There was Colonel Kolkhorst of Exeter. He taught Spanish and served in what John called the 'Royal Portuguese Foot-and-Mouth Marines', and gave sherry parties in his rooms on Sunday mornings. To me these gatherings were the most glittering of all the Oxford parties that raged during this gay period, for the simple reason that being a girl I was never invited. John's fancy nevertheless made the queer unknown don as vivid to me as if he had been one of Lear's fictitious animals. He wrote a ballad about 'The Colonel' of which the last verses went:

There's a home for Colonel Kolkhorst
    With stamps stuck on the sky*
Where the sward is strewn with pansies
    And the services are high.

And there is Walter Pater
    And there is Oscar Wilde,
All quaffing Empire sherry,
    With the Deans and Maurice Child.

Then there was that future dazzling literary critic, Raymond

* A game of sticking stamps on the Colonel's ceiling by throwing up pennies with the stamps balanced on them.

Mortimer. For some reason Maurice had nicknamed him 'Old Mortality' and John would intone:

> In his sulka shirt and charvet tie,
> Old Mortality passes by.

By some merry sleight of hand, John also managed to mingle the literary survivors of the nineties with the fantasies woven around our contemporaries. I remember a soirée he gave for 'Bosie', Oscar Wilde's wayward friend Lord Alfred Douglas. The party I think was held in Wilde's old rooms in Chaplain's Yard at Magdalen, John's own college. The vision of the handsome old man with a stick, holding court in the embrasure of a window, brought a decade of literature to life. It helped me imaginatively when I came to write the biography of Wilfrid Scawen Blunt, a friend of Bosie and Wilde.

'How did I get to that party for Bosie?' I asked John half a century later.

'Oh, you were one of the aesthetes' molls – you and Margaret Lane and Margaret Rawlings.'

Bosie's wife was just as fascinating to John as Bosie himself, not to mention Bosie's father-in-law.

'She was Olive Custance, Colonel Custance's kiddy. He owned a lot of land near Cromer. One day I went for a walk with him; he was a very tall man, enormous. Some bungalows were going up near by. He stooped, as if he had to get down low to see them, and said, "Do people really *live* in those things?"' There was a lovely 'yaffle' from the Garden of Eden, as Betjeman realized that he had transformed a perfectly ordinary tall old man into a puzzled giant, trying to understand the modern Lilliputians.

At this stage I was not fully alive to Betjeman's power of enthusiasm both for things and people. Later I came to realize that there was hardly anyone he did not like, perhaps for their very faults. Maurice started the vogue for praising with a damn – 'I like him, he smells' – but John's affections were transparently genuine and catholic. He became fond of Dick Crossman, for instance, the villain of 'A Hike on the Downs';

> Yes, rub some soap upon your feet!
>   We'll hike round Winchester for weeks –
> Like ancient Britons – just we two –
>   Or more perhaps like ancient Greeks.

'I met Crossman again near Banbury,' says John, 'and liked him very much; he more or less apologized for having been so farouche in the old days.'

It was not till the year after I went down from Oxford that John's special genius came home to me. By this time I was virtually engaged to Frank Pakenham, and that Christmas and summer there were some memorable house-parties at Pakenham Hall, the family seat in Westmeath, Ireland. Anthony Powell fell in love with Frank's sister Violet and later married her. Evelyn Waugh urged me to pursue Frank, and David Cecil, Maurice Bowra and Evelyn's friend Alistair Graham were also staying. John came to both house-parties. He fell upon his host and hostess, Edward and Christine Longford, with the full ardour of his affectionate imagination and built them up into Irish folk-heroes of a Celtic noonday. Actually it was on the comical side of the picture that John worked, for the Longfords were already dedicated to the Gate Theatre, Edward being a gifted playwright and Christine a brilliantly original satirical novelist – 'the funniest woman I've ever known', says John, who indeed fell for everything he met at Pakenham.

With his passion for jokey but kindly nicknames, he delighted in the Pakenhams' name for their favourite uncle, 'Insany' (Lord Dunsany). He specially liked Andrews, the butler, 'a very fierce Welshman'. Andrews once put a stop to Edward's performance, while standing on the sideboard, of the Irish patriotic song 'The West's Awake', by abruptly entering the dining-room with a withering look that would have silenced Dan O'Connell himself.

One afternoon the Rector, Mr Moritz of the Church of Ireland, came up from his local parsonage to tea at 'the Castle'. At once John's ecstatic love affair with Ireland, its Protestant Church and Anglo-Irish nobility burst into flame. In no time he had Edward seated at a somewhat tinny upright piano, specially brought down from the schoolroom into the hall. John rejoiced at the sight of Edward's 'big fat fingers playing very loudly from the *Church of Ireland Hymnal*' (he was the heaviest peer in Ireland after Lord Castlerosse) while the rest of us clustered round warbling the emotive tunes. The two I best recall were 'Dare to be a Daniel' and 'Come let us gather at the River'. I think John's favourite was a kind of holy sea-shanty:

> Will your anchor hold in the storms of life
> When the clouds unfold their weary strife,
> When the strong tides drift and the cables strain,
> Does your anchor shift or firm remain?
>
> *Chorus:* We have an anchor that keeps the soul
> Steadfast and sure while the billows roll.

From the piano we moved under John's guidance to the episcopal churches and Celtic crosses. Edward would raise his vast stetson hat every time we passed a church. On the steps leading up to one wayside Celtic cross John and Edward jointly conducted an impromptu service, each of them draped in one of the white tablecloths brought for our picnic. (John was a marvellous impromptu artiste. At dinner, possibly the same dinner when Edward sang 'The West's Awake', he invented a considerable dialogue between two Shakespearean messengers describing some catastrophe. The voice was vintage Old Vic.)

Was all this a case of guying religion? Far from it. John had brought from the irreverent Oxford of the twenties the secret of laughing and loving at the same time. The more you valued a thing the more you honoured it with something that looked like parody but was in fact profound approval. He was to apply the same formula to Irish actresses and peers. He adored pretty Cathleen

Delaney of the Gate and her husband John O'Day the 'eigoneer' (some obscure joke about engineers); they lived at 16 Waltham Terrace, Blackrock, an ordinary Dublin house, but John always called it 'The Cabin'.

As for the local nobility, 'I cannot imagine a nicer fate,' said John, 'than to be a hereditary Irish peer.' Charles Aloysius, 18th Lord Trimlestown, born 1861, was perhaps the best beloved. 'Why do you like him so much?' I would ask. (At first I had thought him an invention.)

'Because he is so little known. Irish peers are much better than the others . . . I don't like them to be well known.'

Lord Massy was almost a rival of Lord Trimlestown. 'He drove a taxi in Dublin and had a descendant who kept a grocer's shop in Leicester. Just the kind of man I like,' mused John. 'I never met any of them. That was the thing I liked.'

I must try to draw together these influences of fifty years ago. The keynote was satirical enthusiasm that laughs at, even ridicules itself, but is so deep and sincere that it loves its idols' weaknesses as well as their admirable qualities. Of course there is a risk of sentimentality; but you relied on laughter to purge it. Betjeman, being a genius, took colossal risks and got away with it. I think of the first of his *Collected Poems*, 'Death in Leamington'. In my first biography, that of a splendid woman, I tried in a modest way to achieve the same kind of balance. In one sense Queen Victoria had to be my Miss Joan Hunter Dunn.

I was brought up in a serious judgemental climate where righteous indignation played an honoured role. It was a legacy from 'plain living and high thinking' adapted to later generations of Nonconformists. At Oxford I was bowled over to discover the existence of a contrasting culture. Today I can hear in imagination an exuberant 'yaffle' that rings out whenever the tone becomes too pompous or complacent.

Tyrone Guthrie

IAN MCKELLEN

Our family were churchgoers. Grandpa Sutcliffe was a professional; a gentlemanly non-conformist minister in a quiet corner of the north of England. Grandad McKellen, in the same village, was an amateur; a lay-preacher with a charismatic pulpit-style – large gestures from the shoulder like an actor. Reading the nativity story at the primary-school Carol Service was my first attempt at performing in public. But, grown up, I wouldn't be a preacher: I was going to act. Even when I told them I wanted to be a schoolmaster, or a journalist, or a chef, I was planning for the Theatre.

Throughout the middle fifties, with the school camp at Stratford-upon-Avon, I collected all the famous Shakespeare plays and most of the magical Shakespeare actors. Olivier as Macbeth and Malvolio; Gielgud as Lear and Prospero; Peggy Ashcroft's Imogen and Rosalind; and Vanessa Redgrave's. Young O'Toole's noble Shylock; Paul Robeson's third Othello, blundering and bellowing like a wounded elephant. Afterwards, round the camp-stove, I learnt from the masters and the older boys, the game of criticism. The magic was definable. Back home in Bolton, in the programmes of the weekly repertory players, I marked their performances out of ten.

At school, I acted non-stop and envied my contemporaries in films, radio plays and pantomimes, who had preceded me into show-business. I was allowed backstage at the local Grand Theatre, where variety turns held out against the encroaching counter-attraction of television. There, silent and ignored, among the dust, I marvelled as the comics and magicians, the chorus girls and the acrobats, disguised their grinding hard work as glamour on stage. Their sweat shone like stardust. I despaired only that I should ever know enough to shine like them.

At university, everyone was confident. All the undergrad actors were going into the business, dear. I caught their infection chronically. In twenty-one plays at Cambridge, I served my apprenticeship; yet, still, I felt unprepared for the profession. In character roles, made-up in crêpe-hair and padding as Toby Belch, all was promising. But as an unadorned juvenile, as Posthumus Leonatus or as Turgenev's Beliayev, my youth was self-conscious, embarrassed and embarrassing. Imitation, mimicry and caricature were insufficient. Prepared to labour as hard as any pro, I didn't know how to release and reveal my inner life. My acting was all gestures and no heart.

Once down from Cambridge, it was up to Coventry as a junior actor in a fortnightly repertory of thrillers, light and heavy comedies, popular old plays and unpopular new ones. The style for much of this was set by the director of my professional debut, who addressed the first rehearsal: 'O.K., the play's *A Man for All Seasons*. In your scripts, you'll find the moves they did in the West End production – what was good enough for Paul Scofield for over a year will do us very nicely for a couple of weeks.' What it was to be in the Theatre. Learn the lines and don't bump into the furniture. I bumped into a lot of furniture in the next two years but my fellow actors picked up the pieces and were very kind about my arrival from Cambridge. Real pros trained at drama schools. 'Ex-varsity chappies, well, you know, love, they always seem to have rehearsed in front of the mirror.' Which I stopped doing immediately. Oh, how eager to learn: how happy to be rewarded with some rattling good parts. I was getting better and I was getting on.

In 1963, I turned down a job in London (I still wasn't good enough). Instead I went to Nottingham. There, the new playhouse would open with *Coriolanus*: I would play Aufidius: Tyrone Guthrie, the director.

To recall his impact on me, twenty-three years old, there's no need to catalogue his lifetime's achievement. I knew then only a little of his reputation as the brilliant maverick who had run the Old

Vic after the Second World War and then brought excitement to the classical theatre wherever he worked in Britain, Israel, Australia, Canada or at his own custom-built playhouse in Minneapolis. He bestrode world theatre like a Colossus. And he looked like one, even at our damp, autumn rehearsals. Six-feet-three in his galoshes, muffling up a serious cold, hugging himself in an ankle-length tweed overcoat, then stretching out his long arms as he spoke, radiating energy like a sun: 'I'm going to read to you this introduction to an American edition of *Coriolanus*. I agree with every word of it.' This short essay concentrated on Coriolanus's heroism, underpinned or undermined by a mother-fixation. His arch-rival Aufidius was a father/friend figure whom Coriolanus worshipped in combat and lusted after in his dreams. The play, and our production, turned on this homosexual axis. It was a bold interpretation, albeit second-hand. Next day the book was lying on the stage-manager's table '. . . with an introduction by Tyrone Guthrie'.

Another novelty was the design of late eighteenth-century plumes, breastplates, breeches and boots. 'If you're all in togas, the audience will never know who's who. The play only works if they distinguish civilians from military, friends from foreigners, nobility from the mob.' His cast was large and varied – stars, tyros, even amateur actors in the crowd scenes. Anarchy was controlled by a clear, commonsense directive for each scene. For instance, Coriolanus's victorious return from war was to be celebrated with a municipal reception in Rome: crowds roped-off by officials, a red carpet laid, battle trophies paraded – men cheering, women weeping, salutes, handshakes, hugs and kisses. It was a public scene against which the private emotions would be glimpsed. We must all be in it. Aufidius had no part in the scene, so: 'Ian, you'll carry a big banner to hide your face – you won't be recognized and you can help fill the stage with flags.' 'I can see you, Leo McKern, too much funny business with those ropes . . .' Michael Crawford, in his first Shakespeare, accidentally tripped and Guthrie, perhaps, initiated a subsequent career of comic stunts: 'Don't worry; I like the trip, do it again more obviously!' He spied everyone's potential and encouraged it.

Aufidius has a number of short solo speeches, difficult to get right while other actors are waiting to rehearse. So he gently suggested I come in each morning before the rest for private tuition. After a couple of weeks: 'Right, I think you know you're good enough to show the others how hard you've been working.' I would have worked all night if he'd asked it. He despised slacking. The assistant stage-manager, in charge of sound effects, was fresh from an abandoned career with an airline. At the climax of the victory parade, she missed her cue for the peal of bells and the scene jerked to a halt. Guthrie, long arms pointing at her, flapped towards the stage: 'You are an air-hostess and as a result of your carelessness, the whole plane is going down in flames. Do your job properly or kindly leave the stage.'

He was in Nottingham, a compulsive missionary, spreading his gospel that theatre is excitement and entertainment, not 'culture', dread word, nor an escape from life; rather its enhancement. In unfashionable corners of the world, he championed theatre people whose hard work, expertise and imagination might serve their community. We were preachers with a message. I'd never expected that.

After the official opening of the playhouse, we were all to join the civic dignitaries for a reception at the town hall. It might have been staged by Guthrie's sense of humour. By the time we arrived all the food was scoffed and the drink dried up. From within the privileged roped-off Mayoral Parlour, where royalty were still privately feasting, we heard Guthrie berating the Town Clerk who had refused access to the weary, hungry actors. 'All evening long, you have been entertained by these people who have worked for weeks, all hours for little pay, presenting your town with their magnificent talents. And your reward is to spurn them. This is not seemly.' The Colossus flapped out past the drinks table, removed a tray of gin and tonics and, genuinely indignant, distributed them to us outside.

The next day he flew on to more excitement in America.

He had changed my life, two days before, at the dress rehearsal. Aufidius slaughters his beloved enemy Coriolanus and then ends the play with a speech that many actors (including me) might interpret as mere hypocrisy:

> My rage is gone,
> And I am struck with sorrow . . .

Guthrie insisted that it was heartfelt and that it be preceded by a wail of keening anguish over the corpse. It was a moment I had muffed at each rehearsal and fooled myself that my gestures would distract from my lack of heart. I was embarrassed. I was acting badly and now, at the dress rehearsal, was my last chance to get it right. I could still feel nothing. And he said, standing right up against the edge of the stage, privately, but loud enough to be heard – for his message was an unforgettable one: 'We are at the climax of a masterpiece. If we haven't convinced the audience by this time that they are in the presence of a great play, they might as well have stayed at home with the television. Aufidius is a man but he can grow, as we all can, to behave like a god. His rage *can* turn to sorrow. Fill your mind, your imagination with your feelings and let your heart wail. If you can't do it, it's all a waste. You can.'

Those weren't his words precisely but can you understand that at last I knew why acting is difficult and, yet, a glory? It demands that you dare to cut open your heart and make the audience care that you've done it. I think I managed. Of course, it helped that the play was Shakespeare and that the director was Tyrone Guthrie.

An Old Lady

DEREK MAHON

The old motorbike she was
The first woman in those
Parts to ride – a noble
Norton – disintegrates
With rusty iron gates
In some abandoned stable;

But lives in sepia shades
Where an emancipated
Country schoolteacher
Of nineteen thirty-eight
Grins from her frame before
Broaching the mountain roads.

Forty years later she
Shakes slack on the fire
To dowse it while she goes
Into the town to buy
Groceries and newspaper
And exchange courtesies.

Then back to a pot of tea
And the early-evening news
(Some fresh atrocity);
Washes up to the sound
Of a chat-show, one phrase
Of Bach going round and round

Derek Mahon

In her head as she stares
Out at the wintry moon
And thinks of her daughters
So very far away –
Although the telephone
Makes nonsense of that today.

Out there beyond the edge
Of the golf course tosses
The ghost of the *Girona*,
Flagship of the Armada –
History. Does the knowledge
Alter the world she sees?

Or do her thoughts travel
By preference among
Memories of her naval
Husband, thirty years
Drowned, the water-colours
And instruments unstrung?

A tentatively romantic
Figure once, she became
Merely an old lady like
Many another, with
Her favourite programme
And her sustaining faith.

She sits now and watches
Incredulously as some mad
Whipper-snapper howls
His love-song and the gulls
Snuggle down on the beaches,
The rooks in the churchyard.

A Sweet Shambolic Man

BEL MOONEY

His nickname was 'Bert'. Girls would giggle to see him walking down the corridor, books tucked under his arm, old tweed jacket flapping as he strutted staring straight ahead, or talking to himself. I do not know how old he was, just that he always seemed old – although in fact he took early retirement in 1975 and so in the early sixties he must have been much younger than we thought. Red face with a curious bulbous nose down which his crooked spectacles slipped, full uneven mouth, slightly greasy hair, and clothes which always reeked of his incessant cigarettes – he was a sweet, shambolic man. Sadly he was deaf in one ear and wore a hearing aid which often failed him. Then, in class, it would whine its high note and he, not hearing his own voice properly, would speak more and more loudly while the girls collapsed with laughter upon their desks. Conscious that something was wrong he would fumble inside his shirt to adjust the controls, staring helplessly down at his text and bellowing the lines from *Lear*.

Denis Boulding was the senior English master at Trowbridge Girls' High School when I went there, in 1960, at the age of fourteen. It was an ordinary small-town grammar, separated by a high hedge from the tempting boys' equivalent. Not distinguished, never (in my day) seeing a pupil through Oxbridge entrance, TGHS sent a steady stream to the redbrick universities and teacher training colleges. The rest found jobs easily enough in Wiltshire in those days, and married, and watched a new generation of girls walk to the school in their bottle-green uniforms. Uniform was strict: dark green knickers for gym, and a constant war against the fashionably absurd practice of pinning the green beret vertically and invisibly behind a towering beehive.

In the female staffroom Denis Boulding stood out uncomfortably, though he was eventually joined by meek and ineffectual male teachers of Latin and Religious Instruction. When you first went to the school you were taught English by a firm, brisk lady called Miss Pinton, with dark hair and upswept spectacles. Mr Boulding taught the fifteen-year-olds upwards, and we greeted the information that we were to graduate to him with ribald anticipation. He could not keep control, his hearing aid was always going wrong, sometimes he would lose his temper and nearly *cry* – 'Bert' was always good for a laugh. Even other members of staff might be seen, occasionally, smothering a smile. There was something unique and eccentric about the man that few of them – staff or girls – in that pleasant but unimaginative little school could even approach, let alone understand.

English had always been my best subject, from the time when I printed, in careful pencil, long stories about fairies and princesses. Innumerate, good at Art and Latin, I dreaded Maths and Science lessons with the same fervour that I looked forward to English – and especially, as soon as it became clear, with Mr Boulding. I peered at the world through glasses that rivalled his in thickness, and my life revolved around books, as his did. So we found each other out: that rare and exciting conjunction of teacher and pupil which has the capacity to mould one life, and give much pleasure to the other. But although he was to have the greatest influence upon my attitude to literature, my first recollections are not of the way he taught that, but of how he made me see, for the first time, that writing is hard. Each week he would set a dull essay subject, 'Snow' or 'Time' or whatever, and I would try to turn it into a fantastical tale that he would read aloud to the class the following week. His criticisms of such showing off could be harsh.

I still have those old essay books, in which the handwriting changes week by week and the phrases show the same desperate and self-conscious search for 'style'. He knew what I was doing, and what I needed. So I bridled at the dismissive 'This is very good – of its kind', and sulked at 'Generally very good although you tremble on the verge of sentimentality and must be careful of this'. Once he wrote, 'Am I being too harsh?' and I scrawled 'Yes!' beside it, knowing that he would see but not reprimand. I was sixteen, and tried even harder – to be rewarded by this: 'Very interesting work but overwritten. As I have already suggested, much of this is too self-conscious and literary. Your work would be more effective with a little more restraint, a little less obvious grasping after the unusual word, the striking image. But this is a fault in the right direction.' Thanks, I thought. The lowest mark he ever gave me was for 'an interesting but not really successful experiment in what might be called "sophisticated naivety".' That time he added, 'What have you been reading lately?'

The answer was – everything, but randomly. Harrison Ainsworth, Rider Haggard, Poe, Jane Austen, Aldous Huxley, Salinger, *Peyton Place*, Orwell, *Lolita* (only the titillating bits), and endless verse of the Alice Meynell and Ella Wheeler Wilcox kind. Once (this is hard to believe) I requested Patience Strong for an early school prize, and was refused it by Mr Boulding on the grounds that it would be a bad influence on my writing. He approved my substitution of a Collected Wilfred Owen. Lumbering into that garden of wild flowers he cultivated it, taking me gently on one side and suggesting that I might like to read more Keats than the four or five poems in our anthology, and mentioning that since I had enjoyed *The Mill on the Floss* so much I might pick up one called *Middlemarch*. In class his enthusiasm for his subject illuminated the chalky desks and dogeared texts; he would sit down to *The Nun's Priest's Tale* in front of a class of groaning O-level students as if he were approaching its jokes for the first time. I can picture him now, reading *The Waste Land* aloud to us in his flat voice, explaining it; until I felt all confusion vanish, and there swept over me the mixture of *angst* and recognition which meant that I had moved away from Ella Wheeler Wilcox forever. That is what he did for me: he told me what to read and showed me how to read, and articulated the truth I had already guessed: that through literature you may 'suffer dully all the wrongs of man' – but overcome them too.

I do not know if he could be described, with strict accuracy, as a good teacher. Certainly he would have been better in a Sixth Form College, or even a University, because he found it impossible to cope with any lack of passion for his beloved subject. Sometimes his welling tears of mingled rage and frustration seemed too great for his body to hold, as yet another group of unruly adolescent girls made him their victim. When he found a pupil who responded to him (as I did) he made her the focus of all his teaching, all his affection, so that the others grew irritated at his lack of attention. 'Oh, Bert's in love with you', they would jeer, good-humouredly. It was not that. He simply loved to find someone who loved books, and upon that shared love he would fix his gaze all through the lessons. I sat immediately in front of him. There might have been no one else in the class.

So perhaps not a very good teacher, not to reach those others – but for me he was The Teacher, the only teacher. I adored him, and grew to hate the way he would enter the library to silence the noise of a 'quiet' period, and be totally ignored as he stood expostulating at the door. I wanted to protect him, and lost my temper with girls who took more notice of me, their peer, than him, their teacher. In the sixth form I grew arrogant in the knowledge that our relationship was special, and would saunter down half an hour late, still in my art smock, confident that he would merely ask with indulgence what I had been so busy painting. He loved art. Once when we were about to study *La Musée des Beaux Arts* I went in early to set upon his desk my own American art book which had the Auden printed next to a full colour reproduction of its subject, Breughel's *Icarus*. His beam of delight was extraordinary, and vulnerable.

Instead of hating all this the rest of the A-level group grew tolerant. 'Oh, you and Bert!' they would smile. They grew fond of him too. He was the one who struggled in with an old record player and introduced us to Joan Baez. He played us 'Red Bird': Christopher Logue reciting his versions of Neruda to a backing of the Tony Kinsey Quartet, and we rested our heads upon our arms as the saxophone's melancholy reminded us that we were no longer children. He brought in 'Façade'. Each time he would pull a huge, crumpled and slightly grubby handkerchief from his trouser pocket, and wipe the record carefully, looking mischievous, like a little boy who has just been given a treat, and decided to share it with his friends. We would settle back or loll on our desks, grateful to 'Bert' for his freshness, his enthusiasm, and his precious quality of imagination.

At that age you do not know your teachers; self-centred, you assume that they are simply there to teach you, to get you through exams, and that is all. Hobbies, home life, upbringing, faith, doubt . . . of all that you know nothing. Yet slowly things start to take shape, as 'hints half understood', and the teacher may evolve into a person before your eyes. I saw it first during a light-hearted debate in which I was the Proposer of a fiercely idealistic motion about comprehensive education, and Mr Boulding opposed it. He was, I am afraid, soundly beaten. In ringing tones, giving no quarter, I denounced his 'vested interest', and he nodded meekly, amused but a little hurt too. Of course he was afraid of the inevitable change; his resources were stretched enough, without an influx of 'mixed ability' children, let alone boisterous boys. He did not think literature the preserve of an élite, nor would he have denied less able children good teaching, and exposure to good poetry, drama and fiction. But he did believe in excellence, in literacy, and in what Yeats calls 'the fascination of what's difficult', and he was terrified that all that would go – leaving him stranded, like an ancient whale washed into a concrete car park, peered and laughed at by aliens clutching transistors and candyfloss.

He was, in the true sense, a conservative. He understood the conservatism of Yeats and Eliot, and the reservation which informs the work of the great Victorian 'radical', George Eliot – the fear that apparently desirable change may sweep away, in its destructive current, fragile but essential moral truths. He once pointed out to me that all intellectuals are undemocratic at heart, and it must have been genuinely shattering for him (of the old school which corrects spelling errors by reference to the Latin) when Trowbridge Girls' High did at last merge with the boys' grammar and the boys' and girls' secondary moderns, to become a huge comprehensive school on three sites. He found teaching more and more difficult, and mourned the fact that the 'cherished standards' were slipping away.

Years before that happened, he tried to coach me for Oxford entrance, and was indignant (*their* fault, not mine) when I failed the interview. I felt I had let him down. When I went off instead to read English at University College, London, I kept the photograph of him that I snapped in the yard on the last day of school, pinned up in all my bed-sitting-rooms. His parting gift had been an Oxford Milton – although he knew quite well that I hated the poet. Yet when, at UCL, another good teacher at last managed to reveal to me the beauty and power of *Paradise Lost* and *Samson Agonistes*, I was grateful once again to 'Bert'. He was right in his faith: that if I tried hard I would grow to love that poetry in the end, as he did.

From his home in Bradford-on-Avon he watched my career in journalism and wrote to me from time to time, giving me news of the old school and of his adult children, telling me what he had been reading, asking lively questions about my world, encouraging me to do a part-time M.Phil., and managing (as ever) to combine praise with warning. 'I have watched with mingled admiration and dismay your style and attitude and depth change as you write for the *New Statesman* or *Nova* or the *T.E.S* or whatever. There is nothing degrading in this. I quite honestly believe that at one level good journalism is more important than good creative literature and certainly than academic criticism, if only because it can reach and influence many more people . . . However, you may be in danger of losing your own identity . . . I am sure it will do you nothing but good to do again some disciplined work in which you concentrate *wholly* on your subject without having to make allowances for your temporary audience . . . I think that the necessity of bearing them and their limitations and prejudices in mind is perhaps one of the few real dangers of journalism.' He was always right.

In 1975 he retired at last, worn out by the school. I sent money for the presentation, and one of the long letters he loved to receive, but did not attend the ceremony because I was heavily pregnant. He replied, telling me that he had bought Larkin, Causley, Daiches and a record player with his farewell cheque, and quipping, in one of his little rhymes:

> The Queen regnant
> Is again pregnant,
> 'Yes,' growled the Duke
> – 'by a fluke.'

But at the end of that letter he allowed an uncharacteristically bleak note to creep in. 'I haven't yet had time to be bored, but I regretfully don't see myself doing anything exciting. The "tatters in (my) mortal dress" are so many, and what soul still exists beneath them so weak and meagre, that "to clap its hands and sing", would be beyond its strength. Anyway, it has nothing to sing about.'

He would send love 'to you and your family', and I sent mine back – of course. Yet I did not visit him; it was too far and I was too busy and besides, I did not want to see him in tatters. The excuses you make to yourself are all the crueller for being, in part, valid; you compound your neglect by diminishing your own importance ('He doesn't need me, he has his own family') and so betray all that was. Invited to write about someone who had had a profound influence upon my life I realized that (apart from my parents) I could only choose Mr Boulding – that 'Mr' fixing him forever in my mind as teacher, not friend. The plan was made. I would go away on holiday, and visit him as soon as I returned – to ask him all those questions about his life, to discover what he chose to read in old age, and to tell him that I was moving in the direction he would have chosen. This was to be a small biography, and at last I would know him properly as a person.

Yet it must remain merely a digest of schoolgirl memories, and I must avoid the overwriting and sentimentality he deplored. How else would he want me to write it, but simply? When I returned from my holiday I heard that he had died.

Dr Alec Vidler

MALCOLM MUGGERIDGE

I first met Alec Vidler in 1920 when, at the age of seventeen, I went up to Cambridge, to Selwyn College. He was in his third year, having taken a first in theology, as well as distinguishing himself at games – especially cricket and Rugby football. I was a freshman from a borough secondary school, then something of a novelty at Cambridge, with no sort of taste for games or thirst for academic distinction. The disparity was tremendous, but to my utter amazement I quite soon found myself his friend. Our friendship has lasted without a break for more than sixty years, and will go on, I am sure, until one or other of us dies. Next to my relationship with my wife Kitty, now well past our Golden Wedding, the one with him has been the most enriching of my life.

Of all the people I have known – as a journalist, perhaps an abnormal number and variety – Alec is far and away the most outstanding, in character, in understanding, and in perceptiveness. When I have introduced him to friends and associates of mine who might be expected to miss the very special quality of his mind and soul, invariably they have caught it straightaway. At the same time, it is not easy to convey this special quality in words. For one thing, Alec is an enormously reserved person, not given to talking about himself. Recently his autobiography – *Scenes from a Clerical Life* – was published; an easy and pleasurable read, but telling little or nothing about himself. Kitty said it ought to have been entitled *Alec, Where Art Thou?* This reserve applies even – perhaps especially – to his Christian faith. His admirers and his critics are alike given to speculating as to what, if anything, he specifically believes. One admirer, an American, went so far as to say that, searching through Alec's writings and discourses, the only item in the Creed that he seemed definitely to endorse was that Our Lord suffered under Pontius Pilate. Such facetious speculation worries Alec not at all, and those like myself who know him intimately are well aware that his faith has a strength vastly transcending any mere creedal formulation. When I think of it, Luther's *Ein feste Burg ist unser Gott* comes into my mind. Theologically speaking, he is an Anglican of Anglicans, believing with all his heart and doubting with all his mind – a fascinating blend that has produced a great variety of illustrious individuals, ranging between a saintly George Herbert and a worldly Sydney Smith, as well as its own mysticism and poetry, with, for laureate, the metaphysical poet, John Donne:

> Doubt wisely; in a strange way
> To stand enquiring right is not to stray;
> To sleep or run wrong is. On a huge hill,
> Cragged and steep, Truth stands, and he that will
> Reach her, about must and about must go,
> And what the hill's suddenness resists, win so.

I had been brought up to see the Established Church as a branch of the Conservative Party whose essential purpose was to induce the poor to accept their poverty pending their arrival in Heaven, and to convince them that if they sought to upset the existing status quo they might well find themselves in Hell. A favourite taunt on open-air platforms which always got a laugh was to describe Anglican church services as 'Conservatives at prayer'. In his undergraduate days, and for some time after his ordination, Alec was closely associated with the Anglo-Catholic movement; a dab hand with the censer, prone to address Anglican clergymen as 'Father', and familiar with all the intricacies of liturgical attire. This preoccupation with religious ceremonial faded away with the Anglo-Catholic movement itself, but he remains an accomplished priest who conducts a service and celebrates Communion with great elegance and panache. I should add that during the two terms that he was Mayor of Rye he was similarly adept at his ceremonial duties, and as Dean of King's College, Cambridge, mounted services worthy of the magnificent edifice in which they took place.

In my first long vacation at Cambridge I visited Alec in his Rye home – a thirteenth-century building, once a Friary, where he still resides; now designated for some whimsical reason 'Friars of the Sack'. I have a vivid memory of his mother occupying herself with binding books in a large room on the first floor, probably in its monastic days the Refectory. His father looked after the family shipping business whose office was in a large, and, to me, romantic building conveniently near the River Rother for despatching cargoes of coal by barge. We bathed off Camber Sands, then unbuilt on, played tennis, visited his relatives, including an old grandma in St Leonards who was nearly a hundred. The Vidlers are long-lived; it will surprise me if when I die Alec is not still alive to conduct my funeral.

After my first year at Cambridge Alec moved on to the Theological College at Wells to prepare for ordination, so that we saw little of one another, but corresponded. In a letter of mine which he has kept, I say that I feel sure our friendship will be lifelong. So it has proved to my great joy and benefit. While at Cambridge Alec was closely associated with, and subsequently joined, a religious order for Anglican priests, the Oratory of the Good Shepherd, which had a house in Cambridge. For my last two terms at the university I stayed at this Oratory house. I had not much enjoyed my time at Cambridge; academically I was a failure, the Natural Science Tripos I was supposed to be taking did not interest me, and games, whether to watch or join in, have always bored me. At one point I was inveigled into rowing in one of the Selwyn boats; Alec was our coach, which did not prevent us from being bumped four times – in fact, bumped off the river.

My two terms at the Oratory House, however, were very pleasant; I liked the austere life, the offices that punctuated the day, the talk in the evening with the Oratorians, especially Wilfred Knox, a truly holy man, brother of Ronnie Knox, and of Evoe, my predecessor as editor of *Punch*.

In the afternoons I worked in the garden, and altogether felt pleasantly cut off from the university. Occasionally it occurred to me that a monastic life would suit me well. Even then I had an inner awareness that what we called Western Civilization was cracking up, that another Dark Ages was looming, through which one might live more usefully and dignifiedly if one's only obligations were to God. Let me hasten to add that in practice my life has been woefully far from monkish, though the faith first implanted in me by my friendship with Alec, and implying a sense that the only duties worth bothering about were to God since they encompassed all others, has stayed with me. It is characteristic of Alec that we have never to this day discussed such matters, but, as one learns, there are other and better ways of communicating than with words – clumsy instruments at best, with a beginning and an end, and so incapable of coping with matters like Eternity which never began and cannot end.

Alec himself, of course, took the Oratory of the Good Shepherd vows, including celibacy, and has scrupulously observed them. Whether he has ever regretted having no wife and children, I cannot tell; certainly, he has at times suffered from loneliness, and once he mentioned to me that he might well have been more contented if he had been a Roman Catholic and lived within the well-defined rule of, say, a Franciscan. In purely worldly terms, as a member of the Oratory of the Good Shepherd in its original formation, he might be said to have fallen between two stools, having neither the support of a community life nor the comfort of a vicarage wife and family. I doubt, however, whether he looks at it in this way. Again, it is something we have never discussed.

As a parish priest, he went first to Newcastle as a curate; then to Small Heath, Birmingham. The Bishop of Birmingham at that time, Bishop Barnes, was a Ramsay MacDonald appointment, and what today would be called 'trendy', to whom Alec's Anglo-Catholic ways and doctrinal views were highly distasteful. They carried on a kind of running warfare with one another, which led to Alec's staying on in Small Heath longer than he had intended since he knew that, when he went, his replacement would be of the Bishop's way of thinking. In 1927, back from some two and a half years in India, I took a supply-teaching job in Birmingham, and stayed with Alec in his clergy house, from which I got married. It is a tribute to the reputation Alec has acquired for holiness and charity that when in 1974 the centenary of Bishop Barnes's birth was celebrated in Birmingham, Alec was asked to deliver the address, which he did with grace, generosity and truthfulness.

After Birmingham, Alec became the Warden of St Deiniol's Library at Hawarden for some years, and then a Canon of Windsor. The large house allotted to him in Windsor Castle he filled with what he called his doves – men who had held responsible posts at home and abroad mostly in the services, and, instead of honourable retirement, wished to follow up a vocation for the priesthood. Alec directed their studies, and generally helped to prepare them for ordination. With my family I spent an enjoyable Christmas in Windsor Castle as Alec's guest. By this time Kitty had been taken into our friendship, and now our children and grand-children all love and respect and are wonderfully amused by the venerable figure they call the Doctor.

From Windsor Alec went back to Cambridge, to his last post – Dean of King's – at which he acquitted himself with great distinction, and then retired to Rye, to the house in which he was born, following his father, grandfather and great-grandfather in becoming mayor. I meanwhile had settled nearby with my family in Robertsbridge, so we were able to resume the companionship which had started in 1920. One episode must be mentioned – following together, on behalf of BBC Television, the journeys of the Apostle Paul when he carried the good news of the Incarnation to a sick, bored and collapsing pagan world, thereby founding what we call Christendom or Western Civilization, itself now sick, bored and collapsing. It was a fascinating and sometimes hilarious experience which taught me more about the New Testament than any amount of reading and listening to lectures. Somehow, too, it symbolized our friendship; two pilgrims, one learned and the other ignorant, like Bunyan's making their way through all the hazards of mortal existence without ever quite losing sight of the Celestial City which is their destination.

Such friendships tend to be disparaged today when every human relationship is analysed and dredged for some admixture of self-interest, if not of carnality. I venture to put this particular one forward as in itself, a blessing, a comfort and joy for which I am profoundly and eternally grateful.

What's Your Little Game?

FRANK MUIR

I have a friend called Michael Meyer who is quite clever and can do all sorts of things that are way beyond me, like remembering the names of old cricketers and how many times they managed to run up and down before being asked to leave the field during the Third Test at Old Trafford in 1922, and knowing where you can get a reasonable plate of tagliatelle late on a Sunday night in Uttoxeter, and how to translate Ibsen.

He is an agreeable travelling companion because he does not hurl this stuff at you but, like an angler with his groundbait, has it ready to drop in at a moment's notice should proceedings need a little stimulation. Sometimes it is a matter of dropping in a fact or two which he feels might be of interest (for instance, did you know that August Strindberg was mad on gardening? Mad, yes. But on *gardening*?). At more stressful times, like the occasion when we sat in the Departure Lounge for hours while a man went to find our plane which the authorities had mislaid, he suggests that we play one of his games.

Although my friend's main interests lie in playwriting, cricketeering and looking forward to dinner, his games are always about people. And he always wins.

One of his games (which he won) required one to choose 'Which Career One Would Least Like One's Daughter to be Pre-Eminent In'. My feeble choice was Chartered-Accountancy, a grey area of life about which I know, and wish to know, nothing. Michael had no trouble at all in bettering this. Having a tin-ear and, like Charles Lamb, regarding all music as boring to the point of being a personal affront, he decided that he would least like his daughter Nora to be the World's leading Wagnerian soprano ('All those first nights I would have to sit through – *The Ring of the Niebelungs, Parsifal . . .'*).

It seemed to me that one way in which I could avoid the humiliation of always losing would be to invent a game of my own. I could then work on it secretly so that when an opportunity came to play it I would be forearmed and seemingly dazzling in my inventiveness.

It took me some time to work out my game: about four years. Not full-time, of course, only an hour or so each evening and most Sundays. The chance to spring it upon Michael occurred a little while ago. We were sitting in the White Tower restaurant waiting for a man who did not turn up (he was sitting in the White Elephant restaurant waiting for us), so I seized my chance.

'How about a game to while away the time?' I said. Quite casually but heart thumping.

'All right,' said Michael, 'if you were arrested, mistakenly, on a charge of indecent exposure, who would you *not* choose as a character witness when your case . . .'

'No, no, no!,' I shouted, rather loudly. 'No! Let's play *my* game. I've just thought of one. Now listen carefully. Which eight guests – any nationality, living or dead, or fictional – would you invite to ensure the world's most embarrassingly awful dinner-party?'

I had been working on my list for some months with the aid of *Who's Who*, D.N.B., *Encyclopaedia Britannica* and a friend with a computer and I knew that I had a winner; a group which would sit in sullen silence throughout the meal with nothing in common whatever except an abhorrence of each other and of the whole affair.

'Just off the top of my head,' I said, 'how would conversation flow with Mother Teresa of Calcutta sitting next to Attila the Hun? On the Hun's other side I would put Mrs Mary Whitehouse, then Giovanni Casanova. Next to him would be Queen Victoria, then Dr Crippen, Moll Flanders, and finally a grand gentleman guaranteed to put the mockers on any social occasion beneath his own lofty standards, Lord Curzon.' (I had two spares in reserve, Nicholas Nickleby's mother and Terry Wogan.)

Michael scratched his beard. 'Yes,' he said, 'I see that there might well be an awkward moment or two to begin with. Say – half a minute. Then Mother Teresa, remembering Lord Curzon was once Viceroy of India, would turn to him and they would have a splendid time chatting about poppadums and the colour of the Ganges when the rains came. The ice having been broken, Queen Victoria would graciously acknowledge the existence of Attila the Hun and enjoy a rewarding conversation with him on the sense of destiny which has so frequently stimulated Hunnish races. Moll Flanders, remembering her own robust experiences in America, would have a delightful time telling Dr Crippen what he would have met with had he been a bit cleverer and managed to arrive there. When Queen Victoria turned, Lord Curzon would have the opportunity to discuss with Her Majesty the charm of Scotland and Scottish ghillies, leaving Mrs Whitehouse to charm Attila the Hun and pursue a delightful conversation on how best to persuade a nation to behave as you wish it to behave rather than in the manner in which it wants to behave. Mother Teresa's hospital would be of great interest to Dr Crippen, so naturally they would much enjoy . . .'

'Casanova!' I shouted. 'You've forgotten Casanova! Ha!'

'Not at all,' said Michael. 'After playing footsie with Moll Flanders he would move on to playing thighsy. Having then, as it were, lined up his sleeping arrangements he would by all accounts be perfectly happy just eating steadily.'

I have not given up. I have thought through the problem (as Americans tend to say, as if the problem had a hole in it like a lavatory seat or a mint). The logical conclusion is that I must invent another game but *not play it against Michael Meyer*.

I have the man. Roland Gant. My editor at Heinemann. Likes a game. Won't mind me winning (good author relations). I can play him during a lunch break. And I have the game. It came to me in a moment of inspiration in bed, during a restless night following a curry supper and a television documentary programme demonstrating a leg transplant.

The game is 'What Combination of People Would You Choose to be if You Were Not You?' Give proportions and which bit. Most interesting list wins.

My list. If I were not me, I would like to be:

8% Eric Partridge (his industry and his attitude: 'full speed ahead and damn the academics')

20% Rev. Sydney Smith (the humour and the compassion, not all that eating and political pamphleteering)

25% My Father (died when I was young but was marvellously equable and multi-talented; being ex-marine engineer could turn his hand seemingly to anything. I particularly admired his skill at cutting his own hair, and tap-dancing)

3% Denis Norden (his voice. He cannot sing in a much more interesting way than I cannot)

5% Andrew Carnegie (the money)

5% Arthur Wellesley, 1st Duke of Wellington (it would be nice just now and then not to give a hoot for other people's feelings)

15% Molière (his ability to speak French fluently)

And finally my trump card:

19% Michael Meyer (*his ability to win at games*)
How could I lose?

Postscript

On Thursday, 28 October 1982, between the hours of 12.25 p.m. and 1 o'clock in a small room on the second floor of William Heinemann Ltd., 10 Upper Grosvenor Street, London W1, the game of 'What Combination of People Would You Choose to be if You Were Not You' was played by the author against Roland Gant, Esq. The author lost.

Miss Beatrice May Baker

Headmistress of Badminton School, Bristol, from 1911 to 1946

IRIS MURDOCH

Your genius was a monumental confidence
To which even the word 'courage' seems untrue.
In your *art deco* pastel ambience
You sat, *knowing* what to do.
Pure idealism was what you had to give,
Like no one now *tells* people how to live.

With your thin silver hair and velvet band
And colourless enthusiastic eyes
You waved the passport to a purer land,
A sort of universal Ancient Greece,
Under whose cool and scrutinizing sun
Beauty and Truth and Good were *obviously* one.

Upon your Everest we were to climb,
At first together, later on alone,
To leave our footprints in the snows of time
And glimpse of Good the high and airless cone.
How could we have considered this ascent
Had not our cynic hearts adjudged *you* innocent?

Politics too seemed innocent in that time
When we believed there would be no more war.
How shocked we were to learn that a small one
Was actually *going on* somewhere!
We lived through the jazz age with golden eyes
Reflecting what we thought was the sunrise.

Iris Murdoch

And yet we knew of Hitler and his hell
Before most people did, when all those bright
Jewish girls kept arriving; they were well
Aware of the beginning of the night,
The League of Nations fading in the gloom,
And burning lips of first love, cold so soon.

Restlessly you proclaimed the upward way,
Seeing with clarity the awful stairs,
While we laddered our lisle stockings on the splintery parquet
Kneeling to worship something at morning prayers.
But did you really believe in God,
Quakerish lady? The question is absurd.

Persons and Artists

DAVID PIPER

Other segments of this book have a dimension, which the one that it is my privilege to introduce, does not own: time in motion. They are compositions distilled from the memory-banks of writers, all – or almost all – of whom are happily still very much alive, recalling people whom they have known over a period of time. Those who are recalled in the drawings reproduced in the following pages, are all dead and so are the eyes that saw them living in their restless flesh, and the hands that transformed the interpretation of eyes and brain into two-dimensional images on sheets of paper.

They are fruits of confrontations, in many cases a single confrontation of a mere hour or few hours, between two people who perhaps had never met before and were never to meet again. Some of them are obviously not even attempts at portraiture, but figure studies in which the artist has had no intention of attempting to record the likeness of the sitter in his or her own character, but rather as an actor playing a part, or in a study towards the resolution of a detail in a more complex composition, or perhaps simply primarily as a motif for practice in the draughtsman's art, as it were a five-finger exercise.

They are all, even when clearly intended as likenesses, as one of my children once remarked of a portrait, *deaded*, artists and sitters alike. On the other hand, there they are, the sitters anyway, clearly visible, encapsulated in a precision of physical definition at which the written word only can hint. Whether the definition was, is, accurate, is of course another question. It is, anyway, there; and here; and now.

To pause on them, in the interlude they offer in this volume, the reader must adjust his focus of attention, of eye and mind and indeed imagination. He is no longer carried along on the sequence of the printed lines, the turn of the pages, the evolving story-line. There each image is, finite perhaps at first glance, on its page. In comparison with the verbal portraits, among which they are set, the images may, if the focus is not adjusted, be flicked over as if indeed each one were *deaded*. Readers however are requested to adjust their focus. They miss something, if not.

The drawings are all taken from the resources, wonderfully rich in quality no less than in quantity, of the Print Room in the Ashmolean Museum. There they abide, for most of the time, sepulchred in hygienic solander cases, making rare sorties into the light of day (if acceptably filtered for ultra violet) for special temporary showings, and occasionally resurrected by a visitor to the Print Room, turning them over in their boxes – and may be, from time to time, catching his breath as the controlled explosion latent in the best of these lineaments is fired by his eyes. (Reasonably, visitors complain: why can we not always have these marvellous things open for anyone to see at any time? – to which the answer is not just lack of space, but a tedious reiteration of the deplorable fact that light, by which alone they can live in the live beholder, also destroys – fading the image, staining the paper and ultimately even disintegrating it.) If you are not within reach of the Print Room, you can but know them in reproduction, as here: in that form only can they be immediately consulted, in the embrace of a book to be taken off the shelf like any other book – nevertheless, a resurrection even if not entirely substantial.

The drawings present no particular difficulties of recognition. All are within the post-Renaissance tradition of more or less naturalistic representation, laudable essays at facsimile as far as that is possible in two dimensions, in a convention supported by perspective, modelling and lighting, the validity of which was confirmed, again more or less, by the camera. Were you to look hard at one of those drawings, and then its original were to walk into the room, you would probably recognize the latter as being the former.

The originals will not walk, however, being *deaded*. The mystery is, that their two-dimensional facsimiles – one, two or three hundred years old – can yet live in your eye. That is of course not necessarily any virtue of the subjects: the virtue resides in the artist (but also in our eyes).

The selection offered here is cheerfully biased. Most of the subjects are caught in the bloom of youth. Glimpses of the physical decay, from the trim and supple, athletic, proportions of the ideal human body (as, for example, in Dürer's version of Adam and Eve), hardly appear. George Dance, tracing a likeness on 13 September 1795, seems to me to prophesy in that individual physiognomy a glum scepticism ballasted with dyspepsia for us all as our hair recedes and the flesh sags. (In fact, a remarkably objective comment, that one – it is a self-portrait, materialized in profile by an ingenious conjunction of mirrors.) But generally, this choice offers the exhilarating radiance and promise of youth. The artists do not, as do many of the authors in this volume, trace their subjects into old age. There they sit – Maclise's two little girls, so self-possessed in their charm; so maturely wary of their interrogator, sitting together untouched by time, in their budding beauty on the sofa in June 1828. They give very little away, not even their names – though the artist in his vanity signs his.

Who was the gardener's boy whom James Collinson drew one summer day in the mid nineteenth century, large eyes smudged in the shade of the straw hat, a pot of flowers rich as a fortune in each arm? We know who was that imperiously swelling upright erotic lady whom Fuseli drew – she was his wife, but was he, one wonders, her match? In contrast, there is the magic mysterious innocence of the justly famous self-portrait of the young Samuel Palmer. There are sweetly idealized Victorian images of young womanhood, all innocence and virginal as buds emerging from their clothing. Somehow for me evocative of shipboard seems a luscious image of a girl in a bonnet with her head on a blue cushion – signed by Anne Alma-Tadema, 1902 (daughter of the better known Sir Lawrence,

Victorian visionary of girls dallying naked by baths in Imperial Rome). Lustrous, awaking perhaps from a languorous doze – or is she about to be sick? An earlier drawing is by that consummate master of the individual physiognomy, the greatest miniaturist of the seventeenth century, Samuel Cooper. Long ago, John Woodward suggested it to be 'perhaps the most beautiful individual portrait drawing of the century executed in England'. From that suggestion – unless some masterpiece, thus far unrecorded, should emerge – I would delete only the 'perhaps'. Cooper was unsurpassed as a miniature painter in his ability to combine the minutest particularities of an individual face with a remarkably bold, almost free, handling of his pigments. Drawings by him are rare, but in this one especially, the subtlety of characterization is in no way diluted by the freedom of the handling of the black chalk. It is a masterpiece of economy, from which an unique and haunting personality, of a boy on the brink of manhood, questioning life in himself, looks into you. It suggests very much the scrutiny of a self-portrait, but it is not. On the back, the sitter wrote '. . . *drawne for mee . . . by the greate, (tho' little) limner, the then famous Mr Cooper of Covent Garden, when I was eighteen years of age'*. And signed: *Thomas Alcock preceptor*. Perhaps he was the 'gentleman' of the same name 'of the parish of St Margaret Westminster' who died in late 1699. But what happened to the owner of that face before that? What did life do to him in the course of his mundane preceptory? So particular, so essentially himself, he is nevertheless in more or less degree a different character to everyone who sees him. The possibilities, the pasts and futures, latent in all these images of people are endless – but that would be another book, of Imaginary Lives.

119

1　Anna Alma-Tadema (1885–1943), *Girl in a Bonnet with her Head on a Blue Pillow*. Water-colour

2 Daniel Maclise (1806–1870), *Two Girls seated on a Sofa.*
   Water-colour over pencil

3 Sir Hubert von Herkomer (1849–1914), *A Tyrolean Boy in a Hat Resting*. Black chalk

4 William Hatherell (1855–1928), *Girl Sketching*. Black ink

5 James Collinson (1825–1881), *The Gardener's Boy*. Water and body
colours, varnished

6 William Lee (1810–1865), *Portrait of a Little Girl Writing.*
Oil on panel

7 Thomas Gainsborough (1727–1788), *Study of a Woman, seen from the Back*. Black chalk and stump, heightened with white

8 Daniel Maclise (1806–1870), *A Young Man seated in a Chair*.
Water-colour over pencil

9 Samuel Cooper (1609–1672), *Portrait of Thomas Alcock*. Black chalk,
   heightened with white

10 George Dance II (1741–1825), *Portrait of the Artist*. Pencil

11 Jonathan Richardson I (1665–1745), *Head of a Man*. Black and white chalks

12 Samuel Palmer (1805–1881), *Self-Portait*. Black and white chalk

13 Henry Fuseli (1741–1825), *Portrait of Mrs Fuseli*. Water-colour

14 Walter Richard Sickert (1860–1942), *Full-length portrait of Mrs William Hulton*. Black and coloured chalks

15 Robert Collinson (1832–c. 1889), *Ordered on Foreign Service.*
Oil on canvas

Five Foxian Fragments

GERALD PRIESTLAND

Based upon incidents in the life of George Fox,
founder of the Quakers.

1

I see George Fox as the hero who –
Riding the open range in his leather britches –
Is the most nonviolent cowboy in the West;
But tougher than any gunslinger, handsomer too.
The image comes from his Journal, where Margaret Fell
'Had a vision of a man in a white hat'.
That was George, the Good Guy. But I wish,
Somewhere, he'd left us the name of his horse.

2

1649, it was. Just out of Nottingham jail,
Fox rode into one of those peasant tableaux:
A madwoman (half the village holding her down) being bled by a
    surgeon.
Fat lot of use! 'Let her go!'
Then, says George, 'In the Lord's name, Peace! And be still!'
And she was.
Bloodletting never did anything for madness.
Never will.

135

3

Locked in Carlisle (where they had sworn to hang him
But dared not),
Baited like a bear,
Fox started to sing psalms in the Lord's power.
To shut him up – and knowing he was a saint
Drawn off from vain delights like dancing – the jailer
Produced a fiddler, calculating
His reels and jigs would throw George off his stride,
Making a hoedown of his holiness.
Fox roared the fiddler to a fullstop,
Psalmed him to silence.
(And yet, just once, I would have liked to see George dance.)

4

Fox rode soberly out of Weymouth,
With a jolly captain by his side;
'The fattest, merriest, cheerfullest man
And most given to laughter that ever I met.'
He laughed at everything; and the more
He laughed, the more
Fox spoke of the dreadful power of the Lord.
It took delayed effect. Next time they met
The captain was a serious, godly man, set
In the Truth. 'And left his laughing,' says George.
Amen. But what a pity.

5

Shut up in Derby, George unloosed
A quiver of letters at all within range:
To priests and judges, magistrates,
The mayor, the town in general:

'O Derby, it doth break my heart to see
How God is dishonoured in thee,
O Derby!' And he wrote also
To the ringers who rang in St Peter's steeplehouse,
Telling: 'Beware of pleasures,
And prize your time.
For the time will come
When you will say
You had time – when it is past!'
(George wrote to the ringers):
'Oh, consider
How time is precious!'
They rang on, regardless.

A Temporary Master

ANTHONY QUINTON

I arrived as a new boy shortly after the outbreak of war in September 1939, in my mother's embarrassingly small and elderly car – a Wolseley Hornet about three years old. The school, Stowe, was in Buckinghamshire, a neglected ducal mansion given a new coat of paint here and there and supplied with various educational appurtenances: games fields, classrooms of various levels of improvisation, a fairly grand and hideous chapel.

The boys proved to be a pretty reasonable crew on the whole, with a pleasant leaning to weirdness of background, appearance and character, so that the solid core of straightforward, clean-cut British lads was mitigated by a kind of decorative fringe. The masters with a few exceptions were not too bad either, although that was a less important consideration. One of the contingent mercies of war soon began to reveal itself as the more physical and oppressive of the masters volunteered or were called up. A delightful side-effect was that the Officers Training Corps came to be officered by some magnificently unsuitable figures, as apt for the heroic roles thrust on them as the average operatic tenor. Another was the arrival of some replacements for the departed warriors, men in no danger of being called up and without any direct or, at any rate, recent experience of schoolteaching.

The most colourful of these was Professor G. Wilson Knight, the distinguished Shakespearean critic, with rolling eyes and wildly flying black hair. To be taught by him was to attend a master-class by Macready. He was a splendid and kindly man, but too remote in his empyrean of romantic speculation for us to enter into much closer relations with him than we might have had with the Aurora Borealis or some other glorious natural phenomenon. Then there was a very tall, long-legged, deep-voiced, lugubrious-looking adherent of Dr Leavis, always attended by an equally long-legged and lugubrious-looking dog. He was an extremely intelligent man, an excellent teacher, firm but not brutal with our self-expressive nonsense, an adroit user of silence to bring home to one who had just spoken the fatuity of what he had just said. He had been on the staff of a teachers' training college (perhaps an old-fashioned one) and knew what he was up to. He improved, but he did not exactly inspire.

That task was reserved for John Davenport. I have just found out that he did not arrive in the school until the autumn of 1941, by which time I had been in the place for two years – making friends, discarding them and being discarded by them, keeping safely clear of the action on the Rugby field, messing about, scrounging for food and love. But I recall only a brief period of preliminary orientation, as it were, during which he was not present.

At that time he was thirty-five years old and looked much as he did for the rest of his life. He was quite short and very round, but in an entirely unflabby way. (He had boxed at Cambridge and possibly won a blue, or half-blue, for doing so.) His head was perfectly spherical but the face not at all bad-looking in a genially tough sort of way: with large eyes, a quite symmetrically flattened boxer's nose, a wide usually smiling mouth, dark brown hair swept back in some abundance and without a parting. His was, I think, more a French than an English physical type: his bulk being the outcome of steady self-indulgence, not of glandular disorder. He was Oscar Homolka without the threat of central European brutality; a middle-period Orson Welles miniaturized to some extent.

His effect on the school community, and particularly on my self-consciously 'intellectual' part of it, was considerable. He took over the school library – housed in a vast and noble room but a little inert as an institution – and soon filled it with splendid things, soaring over the permitted budget in a way which was, it proved, standard procedure for him. I remember a conspicuously handsome edition of Kierkegaard's *Journals* which were, or appeared to be, in a leaf-green buckram binding and which struck me as having achieved an ideal physical embodiment, one of his extravagances.

I do not remember being in classes of his where anything but English or History were studied and these in recollection tend to flow indiscriminately into one another. Presumably it was in a history period that, talking of the early eighteenth century, an epoch in which the ducal mansion had been a political and literary centre, he referred, to our amazement and gratification, to Henry St John, author of *The Idea of a Patriot King*, as 'Bullingbwook'. How ineffably enlightened and classy that seemed, especially as delivered in his rather high, reedy, penetrating voice.

His looks, his voice and his manner proclaimed someone out of the ordinary. So it was no surprise that he seemed to know everything worth knowing, that is to say literature, art, music, left-wing politics, Europe, even films. And he was willing to share this knowledge. I recall with a pang a vast book list of numerous pages, written in his elegant hand, in which every word seemed like a practised ceremonial signature. In it the heroes and clowns of modernism, Henry James and Cocteau, Rimbaud and Tristan Tzara, Thomas Mann and E. E. Cummings lay alongside the heavy artillery of British humanistic learning such as Tovey, Collingwood and Frazer, as well as such lightly-armed *franc-tireurs* as Clive Bell and Osbert Sitwell. It was a complete reading-list for a serious *Horizon*-subscriber, much more inclusive than Cyril Connolly's own book-list, *The Modern Movement*.

It is painful to recall this list because it soon slipped out of my hands. Perhaps it was never for long in them. It may have been constructed for somebody else. It is just possible that he kept it himself. It would, at any rate, be instructive to look at it now.

He was endlessly willing to talk with us about the marvellous personages on this list, and in the associated world of art and music. The curriculum was healthily designed so as not to leave too much free time on our hands, but it erred accommodatingly on the side of freedom. It was quite usual to go along after the evening meal to the curious room he occupied at the edge of a ducal chaos of boiler-houses and coal-heaps at one edge of the palatial system and chatter away for a couple of hours with him and other interested parties. Beer was served in the early days, but, coming to the notice of a higher authority, this practice was, I think, quietly shelved.

It has to be admitted that a great part of the charm of the view from the magic casements he eased open lay for me, and I suspect several others, in the culture-heroes it contained whom he actually knew in person, rather than in the larger figures he simply knew about. Pretty well all the leading men of the thirties were there – Auden, Isherwood, Spender, Empson, Connolly, Orwell. At first we swallowed all this at face value. In due course there were suggestions that at some time, not too far in the future, he would get Stephen or Bill or Siwwil to 'come down'. When nobody did come down a vein of scepticism began to develop. It was held in check by such things as the line devoted to him in Auden and MacNeice's *Letters from Iceland*, in their 'Last Will and Testament': 'And to John Davenport a permanent job to hold'. There was also the fact of his co-editing some anthology of Cambridge poetry with Empson in the early thirties.

In fact he did know the people he talked about so enchantingly and informedly and if, in the warmth of our near-religious veneration for them, he may have been led into claiming a closer relationship in some cases than he actually enjoyed, that does not suggest anything at all exceptional in the way of imaginativeness. He knew Dylan Thomas very well indeed. In Paul Ferris's biography he is to be found talking in the late thirties of drinking with Thomas five years before and they kept this up intermittently until the end of Thomas's life in 1953. In the summer of 1940, a year before John Davenport came to my school, they had written a pretty slim volume together, *The Death of the King's Canary*, which was eventually published in 1976. The degree of his closeness to

Augustus John is shown in Michael Holroyd's biography of John. The others he knew well enough to talk about in the way he did, even if their affection for him was much more qualified than he let on. Where the affection existed he might have doubted its power to survive a visit to a public school in war time.

On the whole John Davenport was much more satisfactory as a grown-up among adolescents than as a grown-up among grown-ups. Before the war he had at least had some money, so that all he really had against his more productive contemporaries was the fact of their having made something of their talents in a way that he very obviously had not. With other grown men of his kind he tended towards aggression. After the war, divorced and broke, he revealed a good deal of this. But at my school, where there was nothing much to drink and an atmosphere for him to luxuriate in of almost unqualified admiration from those whose admiration was of interest to him, he had no occasions for wrath or transferred self-hatred. Entirely heterosexual, he lacked one common reason for steamy relationships of love or hate with the young men around him. I, at any rate, recall nothing but appreciative kindness, such criticism as there was being either as of one practitioner to another or being veiled in merciful obliqueness. He must have had an extraordinary tolerance for callowness.

Did he ever 'take games'? I cannot imagine that he did. Despite intimations of Catholic origins he certainly attended chapel, marching up the aisle to turn into his stall in the manner of some short, Mediterranean royalty, of Naples and Sicily perhaps, with his gown swirling behind him. The setting of the school was very beautiful, even under wartime neglect, and he would walk about the more orderly Versailles-like parts of it with one. Occasionally he was to be seen in the company of a large, handsome red-haired woman, a good deal younger than he was. I understood even then that it would have been uncivil to have approached him directly at such a time. One could, however, wander about at a visible distance and, by such means, I got myself introduced. Afterwards he asked

142

me, as something tiresome but understandable between friends, not to mention who she was. Since my memory of her identity is not very confident I can still enjoy the pleasure of honouring this trust. I dare say that, embroiled in divorce proceedings (his wife had gone off with a distinguished musician), he was worried about the King's Proctor.

His teaching methods would probably seem very unremarkable nowadays, but in the early forties they struck us as delightfully fresh and imaginative. One device for getting us going was to invite us to write parodies of writers we were specially involved with, whether in admiration or dislike. I put a great deal of work into what I am still confident was a rather good *imitatio ad absurdum* of Hardy, whom I still love almost as much as I did then, when, in two terms and the holidays between them, I read through the entire 'Wessex edition' with its tissue-covered sepia frontispieces.

He thought it good too, marking it with the word '*bene*' in red ink for transmission to the headmaster as one-quarter of the qualification for a book prize, like the coupon on a package of detergent or milk chocolate. But then, somehow, it got lost, as did the better items submitted to him by others of my generation. It is said that it was he who lost the sole manuscript of William Empson's book on the faces of Buddha, so perhaps he was training on us for something really big in the Mill's housemaid department of literary endeavour. (I am referring to the one who lit the fire with the manuscript of Carlyle's *French Revolution*.)

But as far as I am concerned this was very little to set against the excitement of his knowledge and attention, the quietly implied endorsement of my enthusiasms, the apparently unforced courtesy, the flattering intimacy and lack of condescension he showed when one was with him. I am fairly sure that I was the most naïve and uncritical of his admirers at the time of which I am writing. He was an admirably resourceful and accurate mimic and I dare say he was quite funny about me when I was not on the scene. But he was very good to me. As a foretaste of what was to come, I was a moderately

143

fat boy, a condition about which I was sensitive. By simply being fat and yet so self-confident and so superbly informed and alive John Davenport perhaps proved to me, without my being aware of it, that it was possible to be an outsize fitting and yet to carry it off intellectually. It may be that, consciously or not, he too responded to our physical affinity.

He left the school not long after I did. I had a short, appetizing period at Oxford before being called up. He went to work for the BBC at Bush House. I did not try to sustain a connection that had been made very close by the artificial circumstances of school life. It was as if I did not want an idyll to peter out in the everyday world. It may be too that some unfavourable things about him which I had heard put me on my guard: how he had roughed up some unfortunate old chatterbox in the Savile Club; how he had extracted a good deal of money from a younger contemporary of mine who had more of it than he could effectively manage, for the purpose of setting up a magazine or magazines. In *Lilliput* an article on the 'post-war revival of Chelsea' made him out to be a central figure. He was photographed, pressing at the seams of the kind of pin-stripe suit that he favoured, in the company of some rough, not to say slaggy, women, engaged in the traditional Bohemian task of drinking at a quarter to four in the afternoon.

All the same I did see him from time to time, with a second wife, who killed herself after a while, and with twin sons of great attraction. These were entirely pleasant occasions on which we circled cautiously around anything that might excite emotion. Such as I was, he, as much as anyone, had made me. I did not want my modest successes to excite any sort of envious distress when set beside his continuing lack of success of any sort, however small. The dissipation of his talent over absolutely everything of cultural interest in his age made him a quite ideal introducer of younger people to that rogue-gentlemanly culture of the thirties, which shines with increasing brightness against the deepening twilight of the succeeding decades, at the same time as it prevented him from making any direct contribution to it. I am very grateful.

Charles Williams: in anamnesis

'That which was once Taliessin rides to the barrows of Wales'

ANNE RIDLER

This is a likeness but it does not speak.
　　The words are echoes, the image looks from the wall
Of many minds, kindling in each the spark
　　Of passionate joy, yet silent in them all.
Pupils grow older, but a long-dead master
　　Stands where they parted, ageless on his hill.
The child grows to be father of his father
　　Yet keeps relation, kneels in homage still.

What is the speech of the dead? Words on a page
　　Where Taliessin launched his lines of glory
　　Capture for him a poet's immortality
As every reader wakes them. So the image
　　Speaks through a living mind, as he in life
　　Would use from each the little that each could give.

V. S. Naipaul

PAUL THEROUX

I had been in Africa for a little over three years, writing every day; I was full of ideas, full of books and plans. This was in Uganda. I was a lecturer in the Department of Extra-Mural Studies at Makerere University. We ran weekend courses for adults in upcountry towns (now, most of those adults are dead and their towns burned to the ground). One day, a man on the English Department said, 'V. S. Naipaul is coming next week. He's joining the department. He'll be with us for about six months.'

He never gave a lecture; I don't think he set foot in the department, and towards the end of his term he moved into a hotel in western Kenya. He hated the house he had been given. 'Everybody gets those houses,' a woman told him. He said, 'I'm not everybody.' He refused to put a nameboard on his house; and then he had an idea: 'I'll have a sign saying "Teas" and as you go up the road past the houses you'll see "Smith", "Jones", "Brown", "Teas"!' He was asked to judge a literary competition. None of the entries was good enough for the first or second prize: the single winner got third prize. He had some writing students; he invited them to his house and, one by one, urged them not to write. 'I'm sure your gifts lie in another direction,' Naipaul said, 'but you have wonderful handwriting.' He gave the university's name a Scottish pronunciation, something like *MacArayray*. He said African names baffled him. 'Mah-boya' he said for Mboya, 'Nah-googy' for Ngugi, and an Englishman named Cook he called 'Mah-Cook', because the man wore an African shirt and was full of enthusiasm for bad African poems. Naipaul bought a floppy military hat and a walking stick. He walked around Kampala, frowning. 'See how they make paths everywhere – every park is crisscrossed with paths!' he said. 'They do exactly as they please, that's why they're so happy,' he said of the Africans. 'But the English here are shameless. They're inferior, you know. Most of the men are buggers. That's why they're here.' He liked referring to Ghana as 'The Gold Coast' and Tanzania as 'Tanganyika' and towards the end of his stay in East Africa, when Indians were being persecuted in Kenya and Uganda, he advised the Indian High Commissioner to cable his government urging a punitive mission. 'Anchor a few battleships off Mombasa. Shell the coast. Mah-boya will change his tune.'

I had never met anyone like him. We were introduced at one of Mah-Cook's poetry sessions. Afterwards, Naipaul asked me casually what I had thought of it. 'Awful,' I said, and from that moment we were friends. He analysed my handwriting and found it had merit. I told him how much I enjoyed his books. This pleased him, and if I gave him a line I liked he could give me the next one. He knew his books by heart, having copied them out in longhand two or three times – that was his writing method. He was impressed that I had read so many of his books – no one else in Kampala had. 'No one reads here,' he said. 'They're all inferior. Obote puts a bronze plaque of his face over the Parliament Building and everyone thinks it's wonderful. He's a dictator! This country is slowly turning back into bush!'

He said he found writing torture. This surprised me because his books were humorous and full of ease; the imagery was precise and vivid, the characters completely human. I did not know then that to write well one went slowly, often backwards, and some days nothing at all happened. 'Writing should be transparent,' Naipaul said. But it took great strength and imagination to make light shine through it. I had read *An Area of Darkness*, *The Mystic Masseur* and *Mr Stone and the Knights Companion* and *A House for Mr Biswas*. I admired them and reread them, feeling only discouragement for myself, dismay at seeing my own writing.

I wondered what Naipaul read himself. He showed me his books – two of them, Martial in Latin and the Holy Bible. He tapped the

Bible and said, 'It's frightfully good!'

One day he asked me what I was writing. It was an essay, I said, on cowardice. 'It explains why I feel cowardly.' He looked at it, scrutinized it, asked me why I used this word and not that word, challenged me and suggested I rewrite it. I rewrote it four times. When I was finished he said, 'You should publish it. Send it to a good magazine – forget these little magazines. Don't be a "little-magazine" person. And write something else. Why don't you write something about this dreadful place?'

He was the first good writer I had ever met and he was then, in 1966, working on one of his best books, *The Mimic Men*. It is almost impossible for me to overestimate the importance of Naipaul's friendship then. I was twenty-five, he was thirty-four. He said he felt very old; he seemed very old. 'I'm not interested in meeting any new people,' he said. 'I should never have come here to this bush place. You've been here for three years – you see how writing keeps you sane? If you hadn't been writing you'd have become an infy' – it was his word for inferior – 'like the rest of them.'

His praise mattered, and when he gave advice I took it. He demanded that I look at punctuation, at the shape of a paragraph. 'And you need to be calm to write well. Be detached – detachment is very important. It's not indifference – far from it!'

It was like private tuition – as if, at this crucial time in my life (I had just finished my first novel), he had come all the way to Africa to remind me of what writing really was and to make me aware of what a difficult path I was setting out on. When we were together he was very sensible and exact, and he could be terribly severe: Never do this, never do that. 'Never give a person a second chance,' he said. 'If someone lets you down once, he'll do it again.' He talked often about writing, the pleasures and pains. He was proud of the fact that he had never had another job. The American Farfield Foundation had financed this Uganda trip, but Naipaul said he was losing money by staying.

'At this stage of your life your writing will change from week to week. Just let it – keep writing. Style doesn't matter – it's the vision that's important, and writing from a position of strength.' He was right. I began to notice an improvement, a greater certainty in my writing. It was Naipaul who showed me that Africa was more comedy than tragedy, and that perhaps I should spend more time writing and less time organizing extra-mural classes. He said, 'Never take people more seriously than they take themselves.'

With me he was a generous, rational teacher. But in Kampala his reputation as a crank was growing. 'I hate music,' he said. 'African music is frightful. Just listen to them!' He went around saying that Africans were wasteful and unresourceful: 'Look at the Italians – they can make cheese out of dirt.' Every now and then he shocked a room full of people by describing in detail his punitive mission of Indian gunboats. He claimed that there were very few African writers who were not in some way plagiarists; and several were exposed, but not by Naipaul.

'Those are the ones that frighten me,' I heard him say one day to a Makerere lecturer. He pointed to a long-legged African walking on flapping sandals under the blue-gum trees.

'What about him?' the lecturer asked.

'He's carrying a book,' Naipaul said. 'The ones that carry books scare the hell out of me, man.'

He asked me to take him to a brothel. He sat on the veranda, drinking banana gin and smiling in refusal when a girl came near. He said, 'I see perfect integration here.'

When he finished his novel, he wanted to travel. 'Let's go to Rwanda,' he said. Naipaul had a car, and even a driver, but his driver had let him down in some way and, in a kind of vengeance, Naipaul did the driving and the African driver sat in the back seat, scowling in remorse. In the event we took my car to Rwanda, and I did the driving. One day we took a wrong turn and ended up in the Congo. Border guards detained us. They wore colourful shirts and they carried guns. When they sent us away, Naipaul said, 'Did you see their uniforms? Did you hear their bad French? Let's get out of here.'

We went to Kisenyi, on Lake Kivu. There were a few Indian shopkeepers there. Naipaul talked to them, asking them about business, the future, and were their children going to school? Afterwards, he said, 'They're all dead men.' The hotels were empty except for the large Belgian families which ran them and ate enormous meals, quarrelling and shouting the whole time. Rwanda was still a colonial place, with decaying villas and savage guard dogs. A dog snarled at us one night as we were out walking. Naipaul said, 'What that dog wants is a good kick.'

In Kigali, the dusty capital, the hotels were full. I inquired at the American Embassy and was told that Naipaul and I could use the embassy guest-house. This brought from him a melancholy reflection. 'Look what it means to come from a big powerful country – you Americans are lucky,' he said. 'But I come from a ridiculous little island.'

We had one argument on that trip. I picked up an African who was hitch-hiking. Naipaul had said, 'Let him walk.' But he was in the bush; there was no transport at all. I sometimes hitch-hiked myself. Naipaul was very angry; the African was a lazy, sponging, good-for-nothing, preying on the conscience of an expatriate. But it was my car.

Later in the trip we stopped at a hotel in a remote town. It was the only hotel. Naipaul said, 'I'm not having dinner tonight.' I was surprised – he hadn't eaten anything all day. He said, 'I was here once before. I had a row with the manager. The waiters had dirty uniforms, and one put his thumb in my soup.'

He was fastidious about food, a strict vegetarian. He would not buy food at a market if it was uncovered. He would go hungry rather than eat meat. But he was curious about other people's eating habits, and on one occasion he bought a half pound of fried locusts for his African driver and took delight in watching the African eat them.

He was certain that the Indians in Uganda and Kenya would soon be expelled. He often asked Indians about their prospects in Africa. His questions were always direct and challenging. I was with him once when an Indian in Kampala told Naipaul that he was all right, and he explained that he had an elaborate plan for staying.

I was convinced the man would be safe.

Naipaul shook his head. 'He was lying.'

Doubt, disbelief, scepticism, instinctive mistrust: I had never found these qualities so powerful in a person, and they were allied to a fiercely independent spirit, for his belief in himself and his talent never wavered. He was merciless, solitary, and (one of his favourite words) unassailable. No one had a claim on him. 'I have no masters, no rivals, no employees, no enemies,' he said. 'I don't compete.'

At last, he left East Africa. I stayed for two more years. We remained friends; we had some common interests. It did not matter to me that he never mentioned my books. Once in an interview he was asked which writers he liked. He began by saying, 'It would be easier to say who I don't like – Jane Austen, Henry James . . .'

Nowadays I seldom see him – we have not met for three or four years. But the other day, during the Falklands War, Naipaul made a public statement. 'When the Argentines say they are going to fight to the last drop of blood,' he said, 'it means they are on the point of surrender.'

I laughed! That was the surprising, provocative voice I had heard all those years ago in Africa. He was sometimes wrong, he was often shocking or very funny. He had woken me and made me think.

The Case of Sir Henry Irving

FREDERICK TREVES

I was sitting one morning in my little consulting room seeing patients, as I had sat during many hundreds of uneventful days. I say 'little' consulting room because it was acknowledged to be the smallest in London. It was not much more than a cupboard with a fireplace and a window in it. The window, close to the front door, looked upon the street.

I was making some notes upon the case I had just dismissed when suddenly a hansom cab drew up at the door. It drew up as abruptly as if it had been stopped by a wall. The horse seemed to slide the last few yards on its four iron hoofs. In a moment something appeared to be flung against the front door. I assumed it to be a human being. The electric bell started to ring. An ordinary bell, pulled by a handle, can express emotions, such as haste, violence, anger or extreme diffidence. An electric bell can merely ring and can only express persistence. My nurse was in the hall so the door was opened immediately. I could hear explosive jets of speech, followed by the appearance in my room of a panting, glaring lady who seemed to have been propelled into the room as a missile. I recognized her as the wife of an eminent laryngologist and could see that she was as hurriedly dressed as if she had rushed from a burning house. She panted, 'Come at once. Matter of life andeath. Irving.' Although I had a room full of waiting patients I did come at once, snatched my hat from the nurse and followed the lady as she leapt into the cab like a harlequin through a window.

The horse started, under a fierce crack of the whip, at such a semblance of a gallop as a cab-horse is capable of displaying. It might have been the start for some Olympian race. On the way to the laryngologist's house – it was at no great distance – the lady made such utterances as her condition and the kangaroo-like movements of the cab would permit. Her speech came from her like gushes of water from a hand pump. 'Henry Irving – fearful thing – my husband – spray – throat – nozzle in lung.' I could not ascertain in whose lung the nozzle was nor why it was there, nor to what the nozzle pertained. Before I could make any satisfying enquiry the cab stopped, as if brought against another dead wall, and both the lady and I were nearly thrown onto the back of the alarmed beast. The final words, 'nozzle in lung', were squeezed out of her chest as it collided with the dashboard.

Having freed my hat from the reins and having noticed that the cabman was looking through the trap door with some anxiety, I sprang from the cab after the lady. My jump seemed to carry me, by one and the same movement, up some stone steps, through an open door into a hall and against the body of an ashen man servant.

The servant pushed me, hat and all, through another door into a large room. Not a word was uttered. The door shut behind me like a trap and, obeying an instinct of politeness, I took off my hat. The room was a consulting room. If mine was the smallest in London, this was, I think, the largest.

There were two persons in the room – men. I recognized them as Sir Henry Irving and the laryngologist. They were pacing up and down the room, as if they were taking a walk or engaging in some physical drill. They were not talking; but the laryngologist was grasping the actor by the elbow as if he expected him to fall. They so entirely ignored my existence that I might have been invisible. A further instinct of politeness induced me to join them in their silent walk. This I did, hat in hand, and we three, in a row, made a formal march up and down the room, as if it were the deck of a ship.

To introduce myself I asked what was the matter. Irving looked at me with surprised commiseration and groaned. We continued to walk in correct order and, during our progress from one end of the room to the other, the laryngologist proceeded to speak in jerks. He was far from collected and as breathless as if he had been running instead of walking. He said – as we three stalked to and fro – that Sir Henry was about to produce a new play, *Peter the Great* (here the actor groaned). He was anxious about his throat: the throat was relaxed (another groan): the speaker was spraying the throat when suddenly the metal end of the apparatus became detached and vanished into the body of the patient. Here the actor groaned for the third time and, coming to a standstill, smote himself on the chest and, in a sepulchral voice that might have come from a cavern, said 'in the lung'.

I succeeded in detaching the specialist from his patient and took him aside to learn particulars of the event; whereupon the actor continued his walk. The nozzle, I found, belonged to a throat spray, was of hard metal, was about two inches in length and curved at the end like a hook. It had been inhaled, when detached in the act of spraying, and was probably in the right bronchus. There had been no cough, no pain and indeed no symptom but that of alarm. Now an operation to remove a large foreign body from the bronchus of an elderly man who is not in good health is a procedure of some gravity and attended with varied difficulties. I was uneasy at the prospect and still more as to the result.

I now joined Irving in his walk and tried to comfort him as we paced the room together. It was no easy task as there was little that was comforting to say. Irving replied to me in dramatic measures and in so hollow a tone that he might have been drawing his voice from the spot deep down in the lung where the foreign body lay. I counselled patience. I said that I had recently taken a cherry stone from a child's bronchus with success. Irving turned upon me and, in a voice of tragic irony, exclaimed 'A cherry stone!' as if the foreign substance in his bronchus had been at least a cobble stone.

I stopped walking. I reduced the conversation from broken fragments of speech and dramatic outbursts to commonplace and fairly coherent talk. The outcome was this. Irving must go at once to have an X-ray plate taken of the chest. I would be at hand all day, would keep the laryngologist informed of my hourly movements and would have all things ready. 'All things?' muttered the actor, in a stage aside, 'All things?' as if he would like to have added 'including a coffin'.

I passed an uneasy day haunted by the thought of that hooked piece of metal in the lung. I called regularly at my house, but there was no sign of any catastrophe, no slim telegram on the hall table, no scribbled note on a crumpled paper, no emotion-shaken messenger. I hurried once to the house of the laryngologist but he, shrunken with panic, had heard nothing and knew nothing. His mind was merely an abyss of fear, full of terrible surmises and of lurid despair.

I returned to my house for the last time at 6.30 p.m. The maid said that Sir Henry Irving had called twice. This was somehow disquieting. I asked, with anxiety, how he looked. She – ignorant of the tragedy – said, with languid indifference, 'Oh he looked all right.' 'Had he said anything?' I asked. 'No, only that he would call again at seven o'clock.' I enquired, with earnestness, 'Did he cough?' She replied that he did *not* cough and showed as much surprise as if I had asked her, 'Did he put out his tongue or squint?'

I waited in my room in some suspense. At seven, to the minute, the door bell rang and at once in walked Irving, solemn and stern, as if entering the stage for the closing scene of a tragedy. I grasped him by the arm and enquired how he was. He made no answer; but began to stalk to and fro in my tiny room. Two long strides brought him from the door to the window and two long strides took him back again. He had news, but it was not to be communicated by ordinary talk. The moment was dramatic: the revelation was to be dramatic. He was on the stage. He must act as he would on the stage. My nervous enquiry 'How are you?' remained unanswered. It was not a form of speech in accord with the climax of a great drama.

He took one more stride to the centre of the room and stopped. He was before the footlights; the limelight was upon him. Then he opened his mouth and spoke. He spoke in his stage voice, slow, unnatural, resonant and deep. He thus declaimed. 'I went, as you said, to the photographer. I was shown into an empty dismal room. Oh how dismal! I was alone. I sat down at a table covered with rumpled magazines. I waited. As I sat a horrible pain seized me in the chest.' Here he smote himself on the breast bone, raised his eyes to the ceiling and positively shrieked, as if the pain still gripped him. 'The pain stabbed me like a knife. What should I do? I sprang to my feet. I coughed a hideous cough, a heart-wracking cough and there it was!' As he said these words – in tones worthy of Lady Macbeth – he coughed and, at the same moment, threw upon the floor the very nozzle which he had all the time kept concealed in his hand.

It was superb acting. It was drama made out of nothing more soul-inspiring than a cough, while on the carpet lay the horrible thing. An ordinary man would have said, on entering the room, 'It is all right, I have coughed it up. Look at it!' But Irving could not end the drama like this. The occasion was too precious. The actor before the man.

'All's well that ends well,' I said. 'I am more glad than I can tell you, for I have had an afternoon of intense anxiety.' 'And so have I,' he replied. 'Measure for measure.'

He was a very lovable man and the kindness of his parting speech to me, as he left the house, will never be forgotten.

After his death his son sent me the nozzle as a memento. It remains one of the most interesting relics I possess.

RAJ and JJ

J. C. TREWIN

If RAJ were alive now, he would be about 113. JJ would be a little younger. Not that this matters; for me they are ageless, islanded securely in an upper room remembered from a street long vanished. It was Russell Street in Plymouth; and it will not help you if I say that the office door was fifteen fairly long paces from the junction with old Cornwall Street. Shops, houses, offices disappeared during the blitz on Plymouth more than forty years ago when practically the entire centre of the city, on the landward side of The Hoe, was erased as if it had never existed. Miraculously, though sorely damaged within, the great medieval church of St Andrew remained. So did the Victorian Derry's Clock at what RAJ called gravely 'the omphalos' of Plymouth. But Russell Street, George Street, Bedford Street, where are they now in the city of Royal Parade and Armada Way?

I know simply that, when thinking of modern Plymouth, I impose upon its street-plan an old one unfamiliar to people of early middle age. And at heart I am persuaded that the shabby first-floor room above Russell Street (never a planners' 'major artery') is there inviolate, the editorial core of a Sunday newspaper, the *Western Independent*, that was nothing at all like its successor today. The room, as I see it, is small, it is crowded, and it has not been decorated for years. On its roughly southern side are toppling bookshelves, on the north a basket-grate from which coals are always slipping with a mild dusty flop, and on the west, between fire and window, a high roll-top desk where the editor, RAJ (Robert Alfred John) Walling, sits with his back to the door and to his assistant editor, JJ (James Joseph) Judge. JJ has the untidiest table known to man, Everest-heaped with manuscripts, typescripts, and a deplorable huddle of

157

proofs. A few of these, in some deep crevasse, must – so the office jester says – contain an exclusive despatch from the Battle of Hastings: JJ would have added to the eye-witness account a note on the existing social services.

RAJ and JJ, when I knew them first, had sat there together through four or five years; they would do so for another sixteen. RAJ addressed his colleague as 'Judge'. JJ never used a name when speaking to him. He preferred to preface any observation by a sharp, throat-clearing cough, and RAJ would turn affectionately to listen. They had been friends for well over thirty years when, surprisingly, they worked on a bicycling journal in Coventry. RAJ, who conducted it, was in his mid-twenties, a Devonian from Exeter. JJ, an Irishman, had been in training for the Roman Catholic priesthood. Afterwards RAJ had edited one of the Plymouth daily newspapers, the *Mercury*, which had lost its separate identity at a take-over early in the twenties; JJ had edited its companion evening paper, the *Herald*. Now the pair had met in a final partnership: together for only three days in any week because JJ spent Monday to Wednesday organising the local Council of Social Service which he had founded. RAJ was not invariably in the office; he had begun to write a sequence of civilised thrillers, concealed then as Mystery Stories.

In my mind it is always a Saturday evening in, say, the winter of 1927. RAJ is correcting the proof of his leader or of some important news story hurried down from the reporters' room above. He sprawls sideways at his desk, his long legs stretched towards the fire, usually a half-smile on a face still lean and handsome under a bush of silver hair. Inevitably, a coal slithers into the hearth. 'Listen to this, Judge,' begins RAJ urbanely, swinging round to face his friend who, from a cairn of copy, looks up with a high-pitched sound that is something between a cough and a bark. He is a small man, wearing a grey alpaca jacket, knickerbockers, and what used to be identified as black woollen cycling stockings. He has prominent eyebrows, very red polished-apple cheeks, a stubble of grey moustache, and eyes that either gleam appreciatively, or (can it be a joke?) look puzzled behind thick pebble-glasses, gold-rimmed. As I see them now, they have been established there long before the ancient black marble clock on the mantelshelf first chimed; and they are there yet, RAJ steadily annotating in his beautiful, flexible hand, JJ giving his spluttering cough as some new enormity strikes him in the latest sheet of reporters' copy: often handwritten, permissible in those days and transcribed loyally by compositors out in the regions 'at the back'. The head comp., who doubled with Our Boxing Correspondent, used to write a column of notes every Friday direct on his linotype machine.

RAJ and JJ, an inseparable pairing, controlled what seemed to a very young journalist to be the happiest newspaper office in the land. They derived from a gentler age, and under their influence much of the paper was highly literate. J.C., later Sir John, Squire, Plymouth-born and down from Cambridge, had been trained on RAJ's daily paper: he remembered, in one of his discursive autobiographies, waiting in the small hours for the first edition and his articles astonishingly trimmed and strengthened in print. ('You have the same initials as Squire,' JJ said to me when we were formally introduced. 'Well, it's lucky, I suppose.') 'Q', Sir Arthur Quiller-Couch, was a friend of RAJ; now and again a word would go round the office that he was up from Fowey, and nobody would go near the editorial room during his visit. Others, too: a famous Plymothian, Isaac Foot, sometimes MP for South-East Cornwall, sometimes not, whom RAJ admired for himself and his natural eloquence as much as for his political opinions; and lesser local worthies who came for advice on this matter or the other while JJ, if it were between Thursday and Saturday, sat and listened – perhaps nodding sharply or throwing in a quick-witted sentence ushered by that high barking giggle. Upstairs we knew the times when the room would be empty: when RAJ was at a meeting of the City magistrates of whom he was chairman, or at a Friday noon when he and JJ ('Are you ready, Judge?') would hurry off, talking hard, to the weekly luncheon of the Rotary Club.

I repeat that for me it has to be fairly late on a winter Saturday. No blinds drawn; beneath the window – which must open now upon a misty Elysium – the muted rattle of Russell Street traffic. The young reporters above were glad when their copy rested on RAJ's desk. You never knew what might happen should JJ, at his spring-heeled fussiest, be taking it. Possibly you had been to a routine lecture of no conceivable news-value; but if it had touched any subject distantly concerned with social services, JJ would somehow have been to it himself (he had probably spoken in the discussion, an abrupt spray of comment from a back row). It was no use then to try to fob him off with a paragraph. He would insist on at least half-a-column, and end, no doubt, by writing it himself in an angular, cramped, explosive script, rather like his voice but translated with ease by a veteran 'comp' who had had long experience of him. (During this man's holidays things could be awkward; JJ would probably give a dejected snort and write his piece all over again, in capitals.)

In mid-week you might have been to an amateur dramatic performance – Plymouth bristled with companies – and taken a young critic's liberty of saying that So-and-so was inaudible. Nothing could be so dangerous. One notice appeared on Sunday with a JJ insertion: 'But she was heard well by another member of the audience who was nearer the front than I was.' There was also an occasion when an iconoclast from London had tried, balefully, on a Saturday night to dismiss Shakespeare's authorship in favour of the Earl of Oxford. Next morning the lecture report had a simple heading: 'Who was Shakespeare?/A mad world, my masters.' On Tuesday JJ dropped in at the office, coughing drily: 'I was wrong. It should have been "What fools these mortals be!" but that would not fit.'

The friends would sit on until about one in the small hours of Sunday morning. Their clock would announce that the deadline was past; the caretaker, a former steeplejack, had mended the fire sloppily for the last time; presses were rumbling out at 'the back'; JJ would cram on his cap and walk through a sleeping city, past the great tower of St Andrew's, to his lodgings at Virginia House Settlement, down by the Barbican. RAJ would wait for the first paper. Presently his car, driven by his younger son, would arrive in a dead Russell Street. So back, probably thinking less of the night's work than of his detective, Mr Tolefree, to the outlying village of Plympton St Maurice where he lived. It was there, after a mid-week supper one evening, that he read to me from 'Q's *The Art of Writing*, chuckling softly again and again over the Interlude on Jargon and, especially, the comment on 'All those tears which inundated Lord Hugh Cecil's head were dry in the case of Mr Harold Cox'. 'Poor Mr Cox!' 'Q' had written. 'Left gasping in his aquarium.' 'All of us should read this book, Mr Trewin', said RAJ, shutting it reluctantly. Mr Trewin was seventeen; but neither RAJ nor JJ would have left out the 'Mister'; in Russell Street there was a code of infinite politeness. ('Do you think this is wise, Mr Trewin?' – 'But, Mr Judge, it happened eighty years ago.' – 'Ye-es, Mr Trewin, but I think we should be careful.' We were.)

It makes me sadder to recall the practical joke we played on JJ, though originally it was not meant for him. It was intended for Tommy Allen, our photographer, an amiably pompous, heavily moustached man who also acted in Plymouth for a London news agency. From London, when on holiday and with the approval of the reporters' room, I sent a telegram to Tommy in his agency's name. It said with curt authority: 'Dozmare Pool about to be drained. Tregeagle Limited starting mining operations. Get picture.' This place was a dark and haunted mere on Bodmin Moor, a candidate (though I would not have agreed; Loe Pool, by Helston, seemed more likely) for the lake of Excalibur; Tregeagle was the Cornish giant doomed to bale it with a leaky limpet-shell. By poor luck Tommy brought the telegram straight to the editorial room and to a horrified RAJ and JJ. The draining of Dozmare would be vandalism. JJ and Tommy rushed off immediately in Tommy's sedan-car, with the office driver, for North Cornwall and, at the end of a forty-mile excursion, found absolutely nothing except what Tennyson called 'the ripple washing in the reeds'. How the curiously-matched party got on during the journey there and back we never heard. Tommy's agency disclaimed any knowledge of Dozmare Pool. Ultimately, our charming Lancastrian chief reporter confessed all to RAJ whose sense of humour won. I returned from London to find the business more or less over, though Tommy in future looked at me with acute suspicion. Neither RAJ nor JJ ever mentioned it.

Life in Russell Street was bliss for a young journalist allowed to do almost anything within reason, even if JJ's voice would splinter occasionally on its top note as he considered the most recent terror in a reporter's essay. But he had once seen Irving, so he did not moan at me about too many references to the theatre. I missed everything very much when, after nearly seven years, I left for Fleet Street as RAJ had seen so many reporters leave in the past. ('You may meet Squire, Mr Trewin,' said JJ as we shook hands on that moonlit December night; but, alas, I never did.)

Through the seasons I would hear how Russell Street was faring, and how the *Independent*'s newest young reporter, who before long would be my wife, was getting along with the irruptions of JJ. He had an ingrained trick of snatching the newest page of copy and rushing upstairs with it, talking to himself all the way. Miss Monk, at seventeen, developed the habit of jumping into a cupboard and staying there until he had gone. He never knew; and when we were married he would write to us often in what had come to resemble a deformed Elizabethan secretary-hand, and frequently add an agreeable poem of his own.

I saw RAJ last in the mid-forties. Central Plymouth had been bombed out of knowledge. The *Independent* office had moved temporarily to a terrace on top of North Hill, about a mile from the old building. I was on holiday. RAJ asked me to look in. It was a Wednesday and he was alone; one might have thought that the room, books, fire, the same proofs, had been lifted bodily from Russell Street. 'I am getting on, Mr Trewin,' said RAJ wearily and without preamble – he was then seventy-six – 'How would you like to take my place?' I had never felt so honoured, but at the time it was impossible. We talked for a while, and outside – for he insisted on accompanying me down – he sent his regards to my *Observer* editor, Ivor Brown: 'As quiet as ever, Mr Trewin?' I told him of Lionel Hale's parting shot one evening: 'I'm off for a long silence with Ivor.'

Four years later RAJ had died, just after the publication of his last Tolefree novel. JJ survived him until 1954. Now all that is left is an exact memory of the Russell Street room on a winter night. 'Just listen to this, Judge.' An answering appreciative bark; RAJ, stabbing at the fire with a bent poker, turns back to his proof, and most of the mixed papers on JJ's table slide, rustling but unheeded, to the floor.

Earl Mountbatten of Burma

H.R.H. THE PRINCE OF WALES

He was, above all, a family man. He was a devoted husband, a deeply affectionate and enlightened father, a wonderful grandfather and a very special great uncle. He was a man for whom blood was thicker than water – a fact which helped to make him the natural centre of the family and a patriarchal figure who provided advice, frank criticism and boundless affection for all those members of his widespread family, with whom he kept in close touch. It was actually quite frightening to learn how much he knew about his relations' breeding through his authorship of a most complicated genealogical *tour de force*, known as the family relationship tables.

These tables were one of the results of a constantly active brain which was never allowed a moment's rest. There was always a new challenge to be overcome, fresh projects to be set in motion, more opposition to be defeated – each was pursued with a relentless and almost irresistible single-mindedness of purpose. Sometimes the approach could be compared to that of a steamroller, where anything in the path tended to be flattened, but what distinguished him as a noble character was his ability to see the point and withdraw if you had the courage to stand up to him and he could see that you meant business. One of his greatest qualities was his willingness to listen to the opposite point of view, or several different views, and then make a decision based on what seemed to him to be the most reasonable course. In this he was helped by a progressive outlook, inherited from his parents, which influenced so many of his ideas and decisions. But he also made a conscious effort to listen to the more left wing approach and made sure that there was someone on his staff, particularly in South-east Asia and

India, who could provide him with such advice – even if he didn't feel obliged to take it.

Although he could certainly be ruthless with people when the occasion demanded, his infectious enthusiasm, his sheer capacity for hard work, his wit made him an irresistible leader among men. People who served under him or worked on his various staffs invariably adored him. And why? Because I believe that above all else he was honest. He was devastatingly frank with people. There was never any doubt as to where you stood – you always knew what he thought about you, whether it was complimentary or rude. That quality of real moral courage, of being able to face unpleasant tasks that need to be done – and yet to be fair and consistent – is a rare quality indeed. But he had it in abundance and that, I think, is one of the reasons why people would have followed him into hell; if he had explained the point of such an expedition . . . It is also one of the reasons why I adored him and why so many of us miss him so dreadfully now. Another reason was his unique capacity for open-mindedness. There seemed to be nothing he could not cope with or could not understand. This again is a precious quality, where so often people's judgement and wisdom seem to be clouded by various forms of prejudice. Lord Mountbatten was certainly a man of wisdom, of practicality and common sense, but he also had a wonderful flair for the unconventional and a gift for original thought – hence his enthusiastic support for some unusual ideas and inventions while he was Chief of Combined Operations. One of the most brilliant of the schemes he helped inspire and fight for was PLUTO – or pipeline under the ocean: a scheme which together with the Mulberry Harbours made the invasion of Europe a success. This imaginative and unconventional approach made it possible for him to appreciate the metaphysical aspects of the universe around us and to become fascinated by so many unexplained phenomena – particularly unidentified flying objects.

Perhaps one of the most distinctive features of his life was the way in which virtually everything he attempted was a success. He excelled – and he excelled because he was a true professional. Nothing he did was ever done without vast application and effort – perhaps *that* much more effort than most other people were prepared to make. As a result he was pretty nearly always right and didn't hesitate to say so. That apparent conceit and arrogance annoyed some people, but in a strange way he was big enough to carry it off because it was an adjunct of his honesty – above all his honesty to himself. The fact that he was such a civilized and humane character I am sure stemmed from his knowledge of himself. There is no doubt that in many ways he was a showman, but his genuineness always shone through in terms of his concern for the individual and his ability to communicate with anyone. There can surely be no finer tribute to a man that so many people loved him, thought of him as a hero and admired him for his humanity to the 'ordinary' individual. I know this is true for I myself received over 2,500 letters after Lord Mountbatten's death and so many expressed the feeling that he somehow belonged to them and understood them.

This sentiment formed a thread which ran through the whole tapestry of his life – from the Invergordon mutiny (when one of the chief ringleaders acknowledged that if more officers had been like Lord Mountbatten there would never have been a mutiny) to HMS *Kelly*, to the South-east Burma command and Asia, to India and finally to the United World Colleges movement which filled the last ten years of his existence. *It is* for his achievements in South-east Asia, in India and with the United World Colleges that he most wanted to be remembered. In South-east Asia he brought, as Sir Winston Churchill said, 'a young and vigorous mind into this lethargic and stagnant Indian scene'. And it was through his far-sighted vision that he recognized the aspirations of the Burmese for their independence when others were determined to bring·them back under colonial rule. In the end he was bitterly disappointed that he had not been able to exert his influence enough to prevent the Burmese leaving the Commonwealth when they finally achieved independence. In India his achievement was immense and because he had plenipotentiary powers he was able to ensure that India remained within the Commonwealth in an atmosphere of trust and friendship instead of recrimination and bitterness. His personal success was exceptional. He brought a true sympathy and insight into the problems of the Indian people and won a lasting place in their affections by the informality and friendship of himself and his wife. The United World Colleges movement was a particular passion of his in the final years because he saw within the scheme a means of bringing peace and international understanding through students from many countries to a world that he had seen pull itself to pieces twice in twenty-five years. He worked long and hard to establish something special for which he held a passionate conviction.

After fifty years of service to the Royal Navy that he loved and after defending his country in two world wars he, a man who was desperately trying to sow the seeds of peace for future generations, was finally murdered. Rarely have the immortal words of Laurence Binyon been more appropriate – 'They shall grow not old as we that are left grow old. Age shall not weary them, nor the years condemn. At the going down of the sun and in the morning – we will remember them.'

Douglas Woodruff

AUBERON WAUGH

Douglas Woodruff, the great journalist and Christian polymath, died on 9 March 1978. Of that there is no doubt whatever. His biographer, Mary Craig, describes him as having been born on 8 May 1897, in Wimbledon, and this date at least seems to have received some sort of official approval when he celebrated his eightieth birthday on 8 May 1977 at Marcham Priory, Abingdon, surrounded by his friends – still chirpy as a sparrow but by now also blind as a bat. My father, who knew and loved him for many years, always swore he was much older, and appointed a house in Somerset – Norton Manor, Norton FitzWarren – to be venerated as his birthplace without attaching any date to the happy event. This is now the officers' mess of the Junior Leaders squadron of the Royal Corps of Transport. The Leaders may well be puzzled to receive visitors demanding to pay homage at the shrine, particularly if there is no truth in the theory.

They met at Oxford in the early twenties when, by my father's account, Douglas was already a very, very old man. He had spent the Great War – again by my father's account – as Dutch consul in Dover. His biographer suggests he was British vice-consul in Amsterdam, which is much the same thing. As an undergraduate, he already gave the impression, described by W. J. Igoe, of having been a familiar of the Emperor Constantine and St Thomas More. In his autobiography, Evelyn Waugh wrote of him:

I have often reflected that, by analogy to the legendary wandering Jew, Douglas Woodruff might be regarded as the Wandering Christian. I can conceive of him as equally at home in Ambrose's Milan, in the library of the medieval scholastics, in the Renaissance universities, in the courts of the Counter Reformation, in the coffee shops of Dryden, or in the Oriel Common Room of the 1940s.

In private conversation, my father maintained that Douglas had indeed been at home in all these places, that he had intrigued at the court of the Byzantine Emperor, rescued much of his library from the sack of Alexandria, that his voice had been decisive in settling the great 'filioque' controversy at the Second Council of Nicaea. Their friendship was not without its cooler moments. In many ways they were opposites – Douglas ruminative, gentle, prodigiously knowledgeable with a patient, quiet wit and never bored by anything, my father quick, impetuous, impatient and easily bored. Both were noticeably stout in their middle age. I was not present on the occasion, which was reported to me, when they happened to meet in the Tate Gallery during one of their quarrels. Having glared at Douglas for a moment, my father would only say: 'And how is your poor wife?' On being told she was very well, he walked away, shaking his head sadly.

These rows invariably sprang from some conflicting interpretation of Catholic orthodoxy, or violent disagreement (on my father's side), with something he had read in the *Tablet*, which Douglas edited from 1936 to 1967.

After university, Douglas became a lecturer in nineteenth-century history at the University of Sheffield, taking time off to teach the coalminers at Barnsley. In 1926 he published *Plato's American Republic*, a satire on American life which, according to Mary Craig ('Woodruff at Random', the *Universe*, 1978) caused great offence. Soon afterwards he took a job on Geoffrey Dawson's *Times* as leader writer, staying there ten years with the title of Colonial editor but being chiefly responsible for the Fourth Leaders, which he invented and developed as his own peculiar art form. He worked conscientiously at this task, beavering away for hours to find a suitable subject, and, again according to Mary Craig, would be somewhat irked when Geoffrey Dawson (who took all the credit for these leaders) would request one with a note, 'If you have a spare quarter of an hour . . .'.

Turned down for the editorship of the *Observer* by Nancy Astor on grounds of his Catholicism, he became editor of the Catholic weekly in 1936, determined to apply the standards he had learned on *The Times* – 'as if Major Astor . . . had asked for a Catholic weekly supplement'. He had become a Catholic as a boy, largely under the influence of the children's stories of Robert Hugh Benson ('Come Rack, Come Rope', etc.) although a much greater influence in his maturity was Hilaire Belloc. Unlike Belloc, Douglas was essentially a Conservative, but he shared Belloc's anti-modernism and identification of Europe with the Church. American Catholicism could never be more than a whimsical curiosity, to be smiled at or politely applauded, rather in the manner of a chimpanzees' tea party. Although he claimed to be impressed by the calibre of the Latin American bishops at the Second Vatican Council (of which he attended every session), the whole Council was a profound sorrow to him. With his customary historical perspective, he reckoned it would take a hundred years for the Church to recover from the damage. One of his greatest sorrows was to see the *Tablet*, to which he had devoted thirty-one years of his life, enthusiastically adopt all the errors he had been fighting against as soon as he retired from the editorship. He saw society – and the Church – as being destroyed by barbarians in their midst, but he was too gentle a man ever to conduct a crusade or indulge in polemic. To the end, he preserved a little corner of sanity in a world which was out of true. He detested the new puritanism and the 'social gospel' which tried to find a new role for the church in political activism, but he was not, by nature, a fighter, and wrongheadedness ultimately defeated him.

The years of his editing the *Tablet* were the most glorious in the history of that singularly unregarded journal. This was not because of the particular views he espoused as editor, but because of the prodigious scope of his extraordinary intellect. Nothing bored him, he listened to everything and somehow fitted it all into the pattern of his mind. Although his journalism is usually discussed in terms of his signed column – 'Talking at Random' – it was the unsigned leading article which really set the tone of the whole magazine. This was a weekly *tour d'horizon*, bringing in all the developments of the week's news abroad and at home, endlessly well informed, fitting everything into its historical perspective and, to my young mind at least, infinitely wise.

Although few could spot any obvious affinity between his urbane, well-mannered, rolling style and my own journalism as it appears in the *Spectator, Private Eye* and various other publications, he has always remained my model of what every journalist should aspire to be, in the breadth of his interests and the vast complexity of his understanding. My first memory of him, as a boy, is the awe-inspiring sight of him reading Chesterton's *Lepanto* aloud. I have described him as stout but that word does no justice to the monumental proportions of his figure. As his eyesight failed, he held a book very close to his face, and declaimed in a high, brave shout:

> Strong gongs groaning as the guns boom far
> Don John of Austria is going to the war.

Although always a figure of awe in my childhood, Douglas did not really become a friend until, as a young man, I was cast up in a London hospital for nine months recovering from gunshot wounds received in the army in Cyprus. His wife, Mia, adopted me as one of her numerous good works, calling with delicacies, news and gossip from the outside world, several times a week. Douglas, who was equally interested in anything which was brought to his attention, whether it was brought in by his wife or a cat, or one of his innumerable nephews and nieces, greeted me with the same conversation, the same mixture of anecdote and interrogation, with which he regaled Cardinals, Popes, Princes and schoolboys. I fell immediately under his spell, and was never so flattered as when, later, he would sometimes mention something I had written – often in an obscure American publication – and goodnaturedly turn it on its head.

Our own relationship was not without its ups and downs. I sent him my first novel before publication for his opinion – it was already in proof – and he wrote back urging in the most emphatic terms that I should suppress it. When I disregarded his advice, he hired a Catholic hack (since dead) to attack it violently in the *Tablet*. But he never allowed public disagreement to stand in the way of a private friendship, and remained as warmly hospitable as ever, always benign, always interested, never bored by anything one could tell him.

I think he may have been a saint. Padre Pio certainly received some such intimation when, picking him out from a large crowd at a public audience, he placed his stigmatized hands on Douglas's strange, comedian's head and said, 'This is a good man.' Whether he was a saint or not, he was certainly a good man and a most unusual man, a permanent reminder to those who toil in the same vineyard that journalism need not always be a base profession.

Brother Hugh

STANLEY WELLS

In 1952 I became a teacher in a rather ramshackle private school in Hampshire which had seen better days – and was to see them again. It had been badly hit by the war, which necessitated a move from its own buildings in a south-coast town to a country house of some splendour, situated in two hundred acres of parkland and gardens but ill-suited to the needs of a mixed boarding school. It was a matter of common remark that whereas the headmaster and his family occupied the fine Regency rooms which had formed the nucleus of the great house, the resident teaching staff was accommodated in the former servants' quarters, had the butler's pantry as its combined staff room, dining room, and living room, and taught in Nissen huts which were liable to be boiling hot in summer and bitterly cold in winter.

The school, whose affairs were in a constant state of financial crisis, was kept going largely by the loyalty of a group of teachers who seemed unlikely ever to move away: two sisters engaged originally as governesses for the headmaster's daughters (but for whom the school would have been for boys only); his eldest daughter and her husband; and a short, bicycling lady who taught mathematics and science. Other teachers came and all-too-frequently went, supplemented by visiting specialists: dear, deaf Mr Butcher who taught art; excellent Mr Humphreys – woodwork; and a chap who came up from the village for gym if we were lucky. Most remarkable was a man to whom I became very attached and who – paradoxically, in view of his vocation – was a source of civilized, even worldly companionship in a generally spartan, often stressful environment.

Brother Hugh was short, tubby, round-faced, white-haired, and sixty-ish when I, twenty-two years old, thin, pale, nervous, recently invalided out of a brief period of National Service in the RAF, joined the staff. His appearance was immediately striking: he wore a black cassock and scapula, a blue cord knotted loosely round his stout waist and providing a tassle which he twirled and twizzled in moments of abstraction. His deep voice spoke in accents that were unmistakably those of a man with an upper-class, late nineteenth-century upbringing, even to the use of obsolescent pronunciations: larndry (for 'laundry'); 'erbs with an h that succeeded in being not so much dropped as confidently ignored; gels who obviously belonged to the era of Beerbohm and Wilde. Friar Tuck-like, formally courteous yet genial, a great talker, he was well liked by colleagues and pupils, but at this time he taught – voluntarily – for only a few hours each week. He lived, it seemed, with a group of co-religionists some miles away and had been responsible for running what he called a 'home for wayfaring lads'. Its heyday had been in the Depression, during the thirties; the need had dwindled, he was getting older, and before long he retired altogether from that community and came to live and work at the school. He had a simple bedroom – no more than a cell – in a row of concrete outbuildings; the headmaster permitted him to erect opposite it a wooden cabin which served as a sitting room. To it he brought some furniture, books, pictures, a few personal treasures.

For me, this room became something of a haven. Previously, my leisure time had to be spent either in the small staff-room, where the company was not always congenial, or in my bedroom, which was not designed for comfort. Now, when I was not taking prep, I could join my friend for a chat and a glass of sherry before supper, or, on a wet Sunday afternoon, for tea, crumpets (pikelets to me), and black-cherry jam. And sometimes we would go to the pub at the end of the long school drive, risking the danger of encountering a couple of prefects in the bar.

Gradually I learned something of his story. His father was a military man, colonel of a regiment and a landowner in Devonshire, where Hugh's two sisters still lived. His mother came from one of the great ducal families; he spoke of holidays spent at a castle in Northumberland, a manor house in Shropshire. As a child he was too delicate for a conventional education; after being privately tutored, he studied for a while at the universities of Caen and Heidelberg. He was something of a man-about-town, and had a friendship with Rupert Brooke, of whom he could still scarcely speak without a quiver of the lip. Between the Wars he stood unsuccessfully as a Liberal candidate for Parliament, and for a while ran a cramming establishment at which, so far as I could tell, wealthy but unbright young men received an educational veneer glossy enough to secure for them places in one or other of the two universities which they found socially acceptable. But in the thirties he gave it all up and became a friar. I was never clear what had precipitated the decision: whether an internal crisis, a change of external circumstances, or a combination of both. Since then there had been a vow of poverty, yet he seemed still to have some, if modest, private means.

The circumference of his life had diminished. Now, in term-time it centred on his little wooden hut and occasionally otherwise on his unmarried sisters' Devonshire home. There were other forays outside the school. He was a lay-reader in the Church of England, and from time to time would preach and take services in neighbouring churches. Sometimes I accompanied him, and read a lesson. One cause he passionately espoused: the abolition of capital punishment. He would speak in its interests in a manner that betrayed a profound compassion with the suffering, the underprivileged, the misunderstood. This was the quality that made him a recognizably holy man, rising above barriers of class, upbringing, accent, manner, and age to permit communication with people who could talk to few others. Of course, he was set apart by his garments and his vocation; difficult pupils felt they could confide in him when they could not talk to an ordinary schoolmaster. But this was not the whole story. He had a capacity for understanding, for listening, for conveying a sense of shared humanity. Though women liked and respected him, it was to youths and men that he spoke most readily and deeply.

Besides the work, there were pleasure jaunts. Sometimes, wearying of boarding-school fare, he and I would treat ourselves to Sunday dinner, with a bottle of Moulin-à-Vent or Chateauneuf, in the village hotel. Once or twice a term, when duty obliged neither of us to accompany the boys on the coach that took them to Basingstoke for Saturday morning shopping, we would catch a bus in the other direction and ride to Winchester for lunch in a hotel that retained characteristics of pre-war country-town dignity and comfort. And occasionally there was a trip to London – 'up to town' – with visits to Fortnum's, to Hugh's club, the English-Speaking Union, and, once, tea at Gunter's. So from this unusual man I learned something at once of the Franciscan virtues and of elegant, Edwardian worldliness.

Then, one morning when I took him a cup of tea, he had a short spell of amnesia; a heart-spasm, the doctor said. Some months later he took to his bed with a bad cold; only after a week or more did it emerge that he had suffered a coronary thrombosis. In hospital, diabetes was diagnosed, too. He recovered, and came back to school. I learned to wield a hypodermic syringe, to give him insulin injections, and to perform urine tests. The time came for him to leave the school and retire permanently to his sisters' care. Not long afterwards I left, too, and a year or so later I heard that he had died.

That was over twenty years ago; he is still something of an enigma to me. Once, among his papers, I saw a document which suggested that he had himself invented the order to which he belonged and of which he appeared to be the only representative. Well, I suppose someone has to make up the rules of religious orders, but it seemed a bit odd. Was there, beneath all the sanity, the worldly knowledge and human understanding, a touch of crankiness, an indulgence of fantasy? Or did I fail in not seeking a deeper understanding of his faith? The question still troubles me, occasionally arousing an irrational impulse to visit his grave, as if I might find an answer there.

Waiting to go on

HUGO WILLIAMS

I

I shivered in 1958. I caught a glimpse
of money working and I shut my eyes.
I was a love-sick crammer candidate, reading
poetry under the desk in History,
wondering how to go about my life.
'Write a novel!' Said my father.
'Put everything in! Sell the film rights for a fortune!
Sit up straight!' I sat there, filleting
a chestnut leaf in my lap, not listening.
I wanted to do nothing, urgently.

At his desk, in his dressing gown,
among compliant womenfolk, he seemed
too masterful, too horrified by me.
He banged the table if I tipped my chair.
He couldn't stand my hair. One day,
struggling with a chestnut leaf, I fell over backwards
or the chair-leg broke. I didn't care any more
if poetry was easier than prose. I lay there
in the ruins of a perfectly good chair
and shut my eyes. I had had the faintest idea.

At his desk, in his dressing-room, among
these photographs of my father in costume,
I wonder how to go about his life.
Put everything in? The bankruptcy? The hell?
The little cork-and-leather theatrical

178

'lifts' he used to wear? The blacking for his hair?
Or again: leave everything out? Do nothing,
tip my chair back and stare at him for once,
my lip trembling at forty?
My father bangs the table: 'Sit up straight!'

2

Of course I wanted to be an actor. I had the gold chain
like Alain Delon. I could lift one eyebrow.
I didn't wear any socks.
I came home from France
with a brush-cut and a sketch of myself
and my father said, 'WHAT ARE YOU GOING TO DO?'
'I'll let it grow out', I wanted to say,
'I don't like it any more.'
Wine was his vision of my future, followed by hotels.
'You get your own set of professional carving knives
from somewhere in Smithfield.
It's an investment for life, a form of security.'

I wish I had them now. Work had this
mad glint in its eye, which made me look away.
I practised my draw in the mirror.
'The honeymoon's over', said my father.
'I don't care what you do
so long as it isn't a politician, a poof or a tenor.'
I made a face, scanning the South Downs
for something easier.
On a good day I could see the Chanctonbury Ring
outlined against the horizon.
'I want to be an actor', I said.
My father slapped his knee.

'No you don't', he shouted.
'You don't give a damn about the theatre, or me.
You write poetry. When I was your age
I'd seen every play in London. I read plays for fun.
I wanted passionately to act. Can you say that?'
His widow's peak was like a judge's black cap.
'Acting's showing off', I said to the downs.
'It's the perfect cover for people like us
who can't do anything else.
It's better than nothing, surely?'
I walked in the garden, shaking one of his collars
till it fell to pieces in my hand.

I dried my eyes, but I never did land
the job he was looking for. I stayed where I was,
waiting for a last call to find me
putting on make-up in my dressing-room
– 'Five minutes please, Mr Williams' –
as if I could still go on
and make a start in life. I see the downs even now
like a backdrop to the scene.
I put on different clothes and I see myself in action.
It feels like drawing a gun in slow motion
over and over again. I have the gold chain
like Alain Delon. I can lift one eyebrow.

Jan Morris

SIMON WINCHESTER

On one of my study shelves, wedged between a battered 1953 edition of Munro's *Tables* and B. H. Humble on *The Cuillin of Skye*, is a precious copy of the slim book I picked up, entirely on a whim, one broiling Ugandan afternoon and which, without a doubt, changed my life forever. Eggshell blue boards, one hundred and forty-six pages, a handful of photographs of faraway mountain ranges and snowy cols – as I browsed through the stacks at the British Council's small upcountry library in Fort Portal on that afternoon in August 1966, it must have seemed the ideal book to read in my tent back in the bush: *Coronation Everest*, it was called, by a chap named James Morris.

I was just down from university armed with a degree, of sorts, in geology. A couple of months before, the summer had been all strawberries and punting and a warm, dusty flat above a chemist's in Walton Street; now it was a cramped canvas tent ten miles outside a hamlet called Kyenjojo in the foothills of the Ruwenzori Mountains. It was all an adventure, very much in the best *Boys' Own Paper* tradition: lots of machete-wielding forays into thick jungle, bags of scares about lions, fearful insects and unscrupulous workers – a Great Adventure, but for one thing. The mountains for which, back in Oxford, I had so longed – the great peaks of the Mountains of the Moon – were quite unattainable for me. The thick summer clouds hung over them like cream. No one, least of all a rank amateur like me, could even think of beginning a climb. Such ascents as I was to make that summer were bound between hard covers, and secured in my dreams.

Which is why the James Morris enthralled me. He had been Special Correspondent for *The Times* on the Mount Everest

Expedition of 1953. He was the man responsible for transmitting the news of Hillary and Tenzing's triumph to London in time for the Crowning of Elizabeth II – arguably the brightest jewel in the young Queen's crown on that lowering London day. The story he told, with great economy and elegance – and, above all, with a splendidly fresh sense of fun – was thus a story of sterling success, through which, as he wrote 'the last of the great territorial objectives was reached; the way was clear for earth satellites and moon rockets'.

The book had been published eight years before – and would that I had known! For, in an instant – a moment I will long remember, for I was lying reading, in the orange glow of an East African sunset flooding in through the canvas flaps – I knew how I wanted to spend my life. Not hacking at tracts of murrum with a rusty hammer, hoping for a glint of ore that would enrich some distant mine owner, but writing, for anyone who would pay, about anything that seemed interesting and worthwhile, anywhere in the world. That was what James Morris seemed to have spent his life doing: I wanted to do the same.

I was so sure of it I sat right down at the rickety bamboo table outside the tent and wrote, on a blue Ugandan airmail letter form, to ask Mr Morris how I, too, might become a newspaper reporter and have the kind of adventures he had had in Thyangboche and Namche Bazar, and on the Western Cwm, the South Col and Lhotse Ridge. I addressed the letter to James Morris, Faber and Faber, London, England, dropped it into the Fort Portal post office beside Bhimji's grocery store and wished it Godspeed and a fair wind home.

A reply, postmarked Criccieth, North Wales, arrived ten days later, confounding all the doubts that grew during the waiting time. And what a reply! Far from the polite if slightly curt note of encouragement and best wishes that I had expected, there were fully two pages admonishing, cajoling – even daring me, it seemed – to become a writer. Come back to England, James Morris said: find a job, any job, on a local newspaper, and then write again for advice.

I was lured, hooked and gaffed from that very moment. A few weeks later I was on a northbound jet; six months later I was on a northcountry daily, knuckling under to the harsh routines of junior journalism. It was confusing, foreign, trying, a little depressing even. I sat down at my typewriter on a grey afternoon, staring disconsolately down at the sooty warehouses of Tyneside, and wrote to James once again. Well, I'm here, and it's all your fault. What now?

This is when James shifted, in my perception, from catalyst to mentor. He could well have considered his task complete, his advice heeded, the result none of his business. But he chose otherwise. He wrote another letter, longer than the first, saying how glad he was I had done as he suggested, and then offering words of comfort and counsel, firm enough to read like a sermon. Avoid cynicism, he said; nurture a sense of romance and wonderment; during your brief Northumbrian exile fashion for yourself a niche, a piece of territory, so that you have some control over what you write; take no heed of those who insist you learn the canons of shorthand, or law, or 'newspaper practice'; explore the fascination of your new world, and write again, in six months' time.

I did just as I was bidden. Every few months I would write to James, and he would reply, eager for news of my halting progress. And I, from my vantage point, followed his : I read all his books – *Oxford, Venice, Coast to Coast, The Hashemite Kings, The Presence of Spain,* the first volume of the Imperial trilogy, *Pax Britannica.* I adored them all. This, I now had confirmed, was my hope and ambition – to produce one book as good as these. From Newcastle upon Tyne, in those days, it seemed a distant prospect; but it was a goal, a lodestone pointing over the far horizon.

After a couple of years of our writing back and forth James suggested I try for the *Guardian*, 'a fine newspaper, one that gives writers their head, though I confess I don't read it myself any more. . . .' And so off I went to Cross Street and the land of big-time journalism. Not the Himalayas, perhaps, but Belfast; James's reminder to keep a sense of fine romance before me was trickier than I had once supposed, given the madnesss of the Shankill and the Falls. But I survived, and one memorable day in March 1971, found myself on a brief interlude in the Pen-y-Gwryd Hotel in Snowdonia, just fifteen miles from where all those cheering letters had come, I rang James Morris up – the first time I had ever spoken to him. Could I come over and say hello? Of course, he said, a total delight. To see my protégé after all this time, he said; quite enchanting.

I drove through the moist and leafy lanes of Carnarfonshire to Criccieth, past the memorial to Lloyd George and up the stony path outside Llanystumdwy to the comfortable-looking country house. I stopped before the glass of the front door, rang the bell and then knelt to remove my boots, which were muddy after a day spent tramping around the Idwal Slabs. The door opened and a woman appeared – a handsome figure in a white sweater and jeans. 'Hello,' I said brightly. 'You'll be Mrs Morris.' 'No,' the figure returned. 'I'm James.'

No one had told me. True, there had been a paragraph in *Private Eye,* something about James's appearance when he was spotted at a recent London party. But nothing to suggest to an innocent like me that James had embarked on what we now know to have been his escape from what, for forty-five years, had been a form of wretched imprisonment. Within a few weeks James was Jan. My hero became heroine. If the person who had been a Cavalry officer, a wanderer through the Empty Quarter and a climber on Mount Everest, was not a man but a woman then, I eventually reasoned, so be it; if nothing else, my experience of Jan's changing life offered some early clues to the nonsense which dictated that men should fulfil certain roles, and women others.

Jan was heartened, I like to think, by my complete acceptance of the situation, and that of her other closer friends. Such rejections as there were turned out to cause her no real hurt. She looks back on those months after the ordeal of surgery was over and the mould was set as perhaps the most exhilarating and entertaining of her life. She wrote to me about a year afterwards: she was enjoying, she reported, the ultimate journalistic luxury of having the very best of both worlds and seeing people and things from a whole new set of perspectives. She was quite enthralled.

We met soon after in Washington, DC, where I had been posted. She came to lunch in Chevy Chase. When I met her at the Hilton Hotel, she presented her cheek to be kissed. I suppose there might have been a moment's hesitation on my part, no more. She had eased herself neatly and gracefully into my perceptions, and it is only very rarely that I think of that distant hero-figure of the mountain ranges and the desert wastes. Perhaps, I sometimes suppose, it was the unfashioned Jan Morris – not James at all – who wrote from Wales to the stranger in the Ugandan valley camp; an Everest climber of more traditional mien might well have tossed my note to one side, or dashed off a two-line reply that would have snuffed out my flickering ambition to be a writer before the flame took hold.

We keep in touch, to the extent that is possible: her travels, on assignment for *Rolling Stone*, or *Texas Monthly*, writing for *Encounter*, her books on Wales and Empire and Levantine history, keep her as frequently out of contact as my own travels prevent me from seeing her. She rings and writes often, at unexpected moments, to offer praise or encouragement or support. Very occasionally we meet, often overseas. It is not, I think it only fair to say, a close friendship; it is, perhaps, more a flourishing comradeship, leavened with unforgetting gratitude.

I dedicated my first book – it was about Northern Ireland, written in New Hampshire in 1974 – to Jan; and she has now returned the favour by promising to include me in her fictional evocation of the Levantine fiefdom of Hav, that old walled city enclave on the narrow isthmus jutting into the Mediterranean near where Syria and the Lebanon meet. I am, it seems, to be Her Majesty's Political Agent to the Court of Hav, sometime around 1912. It is all a very long way from the Ruwenzori Mountains, and from the Himalayas too; but it was that common fascination which brought us together, and I suspect it remains at the back of both our minds, one of those fine threads of joined and shared experience and interest that will keep us together for a long while to come.

The contributors – biographical notes

H.R.H. THE PRINCE OF WALES gave the address from which the extract published in this book has been taken at a Memorial Service to Earl Mountbatten of Burma in St Paul's Cathedral on 20 December 1979. The following year, he succeeded Earl Mountbatten, his uncle, as President of the United Atlantic Colleges.

ALLILUEVA, SVETLANA, was born in Moscow in 1926, the daughter of Josef Stalin and Nadya Allilueva. Her mother died when she was six, so she was brought up by various governesses and by an old nurse. After schooling she studied humanities at Moscow University. In 1967 she left Russia for India, and then defected to the United States. She has written two books, *Twenty Letters to a Friend*, a family memoir written in Moscow in 1963, and *Only One Year*, the story of her defection. She has been married three times and has a son (a doctor) and a daughter (a geophysicist), and a teenage, American-born daughter.

BLISHEN, EDWARD, was once drafted into a job – landwork during the Second World War – but otherwise has drifted into them; weekly newspaper reporting, teaching, freelance writing. An incorrigible diarist (continuous since 1934), he has now turned into an incorrigible auto-biographer, with recent volumes entitled, *Sorry, Dad, Shaky Relations* and *Lizzie Pye*. Thinks of himself only as a peg on which to hang a record of the extremely odd experience of being alive since 1920.

BLYTHE, RONALD, is perhaps best known for his study of rural Suffolk village life in the past, *Akenfield*. He has also written *The View in Winter*, a study of old age, and novels and poetry. He edited the previous collection of essays on behalf of Oxfam by Oxford University Press, *Places*, and his most recent book is a volume of personal essays, *From the Headlands* (Chatto and Windus). He lives in the Stour Valley, Essex.

187

The Contributors

CAREY, JOHN, was born in 1934, and has been Merton Professor of English Literature in the University of Oxford since 1976. He is the author of critical studies of Milton, Thackeray, John Donne and Dickens, and is a regular reviewer for the *Sunday Times* book page. His essay 'On the Pleasures of Vegetable Gardening' appeared in the same paper.

CLEVERDON, DOUGLAS, who celebrated his eightieth birthday in 1983, was one of the first and best known of BBC Radio Producers, responsible for numerous legendary Third Programme presentations, including the first performance of Dylan Thomas's *Under Milk Wood*. He has also, since the twenties, been a publisher of fine limited editions of the work of such artists and illustrators as David Jones and Eric Gill.

DRABBLE, MARGARET, who was born in 1939, is one of the best known and widely read women novelists of her generation, and also a literary critic, currently engaged in compiling the *New Oxford Companion to English Literature*. In 1980 she was awarded the CBE for services to literature.

ENRIGHT, D. J., who was awarded the Queen's Gold Medal for Poetry in 1981, has been a university teacher of English literature in this country and abroad, as well as a publisher, and is the author of many volumes of poetry, published since 1953. His *Collected Poems* appeared in 1981.

HILL, SUSAN, was born in 1942, in Scarborough, Yorkshire, and has been a full-time writer of novels, radio plays, criticism and assorted journalism since leaving the University of London in 1963. She is also a frequent broadcaster on radio and television, and several of her short stories have been adapted as television plays. She is married to the Shakespeare scholar, Stanley Wells, and their daughter, Jessica, was born in 1977.

HOLROYD, MICHAEL, is author of acclaimed biographies of Hugh Kingsmill, Lytton Strachey and Augustus John, and is currently working on the life of Bernard Shaw. He has been chairman of the Society of Authors and the National Book League.

HUGHES, TED, is one of Britain's best known and widely popular poets, author of a large number of books for both adults and children, and co-editor, with Seamus Heaney, of an anthology of poetry in English, *The Rattle Bag*. His most recent book of poems is *The River* (1983).

INGRAMS, RICHARD, who has been editor of *Private Eye* magazine since 1963, was born in 1937 and educated at Shrewsbury and University College, Oxford. He is a frequent broadcaster and has edited and written several books, including a number associated with *Private Eye, God's Apology* (an account of the friendship of Hugh Kingsmill, Hesketh Pearson and Malcolm Muggeridge) and one on Romney Marsh. His latest book, written with John Piper, is *Piper's Places: John Piper in England and Wales* (November 1983).

KAVANAGH, P. J., has published five novels and five volumes of poetry; his *Selected Poems* were published in 1982. He is also the author of an account of his early life, *The Perfect Stranger*.

LASKI, MARGHANITA, was appointed Vice-Chairman of the Arts Council in 1982. She is the author of several novels and radio plays, as well as critical and biographical studies of the writers Mrs Ewing, Mrs Molesworth, Frances Hodgson Burnett, Charlotte Yonge, Jane Austen and Kipling. She is a frequent broadcaster and reviewer, and has a particular interest in the detective novel.

LONGFORD, ELIZABETH, was born in 1906, and is the biographer of Wellington, Churchill, Byron and Queen Victoria. She is the wife of Lord Longford and lives in Chelsea and Sussex. Her life of Queen Elizabeth II is published in 1983.

MCKELLEN, IAN, first appeared on the stage professionally in 1961. Since then he has been prominent in the British theatre, on Broadway, in films and on television.

MAHON, DEREK, was born in Belfast in 1941, and educated at Trinity College, Dublin. He is married, with two children, and lives in London, where he works as a journalist and screenwriter. His most recent book of verse is *The Hunt by Night* (OUP, 1982) from which 'An Old Lady' is taken. The old lady in question is the poet's mother-in-law, who lives in Portballintrae, Co. Antrim.

MOONEY, BEL, writes for the *Sunday Times*, and is a regular contributor to magazines, radio and television. She gained a First Class Honours degree in English from University College, London, and is currently working on a study of George Eliot, and a second novel. So far she has published a children's book, a non-fiction book about children and a novel, *The Windsurf Boy*. She is married to Jonathan Dimbleby, and they live near Bath with their two children.

MUGGERIDGE, MALCOLM, began his journalistic career on the *Manchester Guardian* in 1930, and worked subsequently for several newspapers, in this country and as a correspondent abroad. He edited *Punch* for five years in the fifties, when he also made many memorable television appearances as an interviewer. His autobiography *The Chronicles of Wasted Time* describes, among other things, his journey from agnosticism to Christianity, and in 1982 he became a Roman Catholic.

MUIR, FRANK, is best known as a writer, with Denis Norden, of many radio comedy scripts for programmes such as *Take It From Here* in the fifties, and more recently, as a regular panellist on the radio programmes *My Word* and *My Music* and the television game *Call My Bluff*. He has compiled a number of anthologies, and written books for young children, and is currently editing *The Oxford Book of Humorous Prose*. He is a student and collector of English literature of the eighteenth century.

MURDOCH, IRIS, published a volume of poetry, with wood engravings by Reynolds Stone, in 1978, but is best known as a novelist. She has also written books on philosophy, which she taught for many years at Oxford University. She is married to the English scholar and critic, John Bayley.

PIPER, DAVID, is the Director of the Ashmolean Museum, Oxford, which has celebrated its tercentenary in 1983. He became Director in 1967 following similar appointments at the National Portrait Gallery, London and the Fitzwilliam Museum, Cambridge. His many books include *The English Face, The Companion Guide to London* and, his most recent, *The Image of the Poet*. He is married with three children and lives in an Oxfordshire village.

PRIESTLAND, GERALD, was a Foreign Correspondent of the BBC before becoming their Religious Affairs Correspondent, from which post he retired in 1982. He has published collections of his early morning broadcasts on many aspects of religion, and a book based on the programme *Priestland's Progress*, a personal exploration into Christian faith and practice in Great Britain today.

QUINTON, ANTHONY, is President of Trinity College, Oxford, and a philosopher by training and profession. He is a regular book reviewer on a wide range of subjects for a number of journals and newspapers, and his voice is well known on radio, for which he co-chairs the programmes *Round Britain* and *Transatlantic Quiz*. In *Who's Who* he lists his hobbies as 'sedentary pursuits'.

RIDLER, ANNE, has written poetry, plays, and the libretti for three operas, and is the editor of Charles Williams's *Image of the City*, and the poems of Thomas Treherne.

THEROUX, PAUL, is an American writer resident in London. His books are set in Africa, the Far East, America and England, and he is also an indefatigable traveller, and author of two accounts of railway journeys, *The Great Railway Bazaar* and *The Old Patagonian Express*. His critical study of the work of V. S. Naipaul was published in 1972.

TREVES, FREDERICK, (1853–1923), surgeon and author, was born in Dorset and educated at Merchant Taylors School, London. He studied medicine at the London Hospital, with which he was associated throughout his professional life. He was a pioneer in the treatment of abdominal illness, becoming famous in 1902 for operating on King Edward VII to drain an appendiceal abscess. Treves wrote many medical textbooks, but also travel books and essays in which he recorded some of his experiences as an author and surgeon. Some of these recollections were published in his last book, *The Elephant Man and Other Reminiscences*.

TREWIN, J. C., was born in Cornwall in 1908 and has been a dramatic critic and student and chronicler of the English Theatre, past and present, since the early thirties. He has written over forty books about all aspects of the stage, as well as others about Cornwall. He is theatre critic of the *Illustrated London News, The Lady* and the *Birmingham Post* in London.

WAUGH, AUBERON, has been a journalist and book reviewer for numerous magazines and newspapers, including the *Evening Standard*, *Punch*, the *Sunday Telegraph*, *Private Eye* and the *Spectator*. He is also the author of five novels and two collections of essays. He lives, with his wife and four children, in Somerset and France.

WELLS, STANLEY, is the General Editor of the Oxford Shakespeare, and Senior Research Fellow of Balliol College, Oxford. Until 1978 he was Reader in English Literature at the University of Birmingham, and Fellow in charge of the Shakespeare Institute, Stratford-upon-Avon. He is a governor of the Royal Shakespeare Theatre, for which he runs the annual Summer School, and author of several books, of both a scholarly and popular nature, about Shakespeare and the theatre. He is married to Susan Hill, and they live in an Oxfordshire village.

WILLIAMS, HUGO, has published several volumes of poems and two travel books, of one of which he is currently engaged in writing a film treatment, with the director Chris Petit. He is also writing an episodic verse autobiography, starring his father, the actor Hugh Williams.

WINCHESTER, SIMON, a roving foreign correspondent of the *Sunday Times*, has also worked as a journalist for the *Guardian* (in Belfast, Washington and Delhi) and for the *Daily Mail* as American bureau chief. He is a frequent television and radio broadcaster. Jan Morris and he produced a book, *Stones of Empire*, about the buildings of British India, which has also appeared in 1983. He was born in 1944, is married with three children, and lives in Oxford.